D0095881

IF YOU
LIKE

QUENTIN
TARANTINO...

IF YOU LIKE

QUENTIN TARANTINO...

HERE ARE **OVER 200** FILMS,
TV SHOWS, AND OTHER ODDITIES
THAT YOU WILL LOVE

KATHERINE RIFE

AN IMPRINT OF HAL LEONARD CORPORATION

Published in 2012 by Limelight Editions
An Imprint of Hal Leonard Corporation
7777 West Bluemound Road
Milwaukee, WI 53213

Trade Book Division Editorial Offices
33 Plymouth St., Montclair, NJ 07042

Printed in the United States of America

Book design by Michael Kellner

Library of Congress Cataloging-in-Publication Data
Rife, Katie.
 If you like Quentin Tarantino-- : here are over 200 films, tv shows, and other oddities that you will love / Katie Rife.
     p. cm.
 Includes index.
 ISBN 978-0-87910-399-6
 1. Tarantino, Quentin--Criticism and interpretation. I. Title.
 PN1998.3.T358R54 2012
 791.4302'33092--dc23
                          2012026829

www.limelighteditions.com

CONTENTS

Samuel Jackson and John Travolta in *Pulp Ficton*. (Miramax/Photofest)

Introduction

THE INITIATON

> *I think 13-year-old girls will love* Kill Bill. *I want young girls to be able to see it. They're going to love Uma's character, the Bride. They have my permission to buy a ticket for another movie and sneak into* Kill Bill. *That's money I'm okay not making. When I was a kid, I used to go into theaters when they didn't have the name of the movies on the ticket. I'm a theater-sneaker-inner from way back.*
> —QUENTIN TARANTINO, *Playboy* interview, 2003

In the summer of 2004, I was working in a video store in my small college town, rapidly losing interest in my journalism classes in favor of watching movies and talking about them with my coworkers all day. The store I worked at had a strict ID policy, so whenever a baby-faced kid would come up to the counter with *Basic Instinct* or *Jason X* or whatever, I would turn him away.

Except for this one time. One afternoon I was working by myself when two boys with matching bowl cuts (change comes slowly to small-town Ohio) who looked about junior high school age came up to the counter. They were dressed in oversized T-shirts and jean shorts and were nervously grinning at each other. One, slightly taller than the other, was clutching a DVD case close to his chest. He reached up—they clearly hadn't gone through their growth spurts yet—and placed *Kill Bill: Volume 1* on the counter.

"My mom said it was okay," the bigger one said.

I looked at the case, looked down at them, looked around at the empty store. Ah, what the hell, I thought. At least they have good taste.

"Just don't let her see it," I told them. "And bring it back tomorrow." I took their two dollars and waved them around past the metal detector, placing the forbidden slab of plastic in their moist little palms. "Thank you," the smaller one peeped, and they tore off out the door and across the parking lot.

I like to think they had the absolute coolest slumber party of their entire lives that Saturday night and, on Monday morning, excitedly acted out the climactic House of Blue Leaves battle to their friends at school. I like to think they spent the rest of their teen years seeking out all the movies that *Kill Bill* pays tribute to, going deeper and deeper down the rabbit hole of obsessive fandom. But I don't know for sure. I don't even know if they brought it back the next day like I told them to—it was my day off.

When I was in junior high school, *Pulp Fiction* had just come out, and my friends and I were most decidedly not allowed to watch it. But thanks to a permissive video-store clerk or someone's older brother (I don't remember which, but bless them, whoever it was) we got our hands on a VHS copy, which we watched with the sound turned down low, huddled around a TV on the carpeted floor of someone's rec room. My friends were horrified—especially when the Gimp was brought out—but I was enthralled. This was a new world, an adult world, and this type of cool just didn't exist in my blue-collar neighborhood.

And that was it, man.

Quentin Tarantino movies lend themselves exceptionally well to reference and recommendation, because each one is itself a dense collage of references and recommendations. A former video-store clerk himself, Tarantino grew up sneaking into grindhouses and came of age in the video era, when suddenly even the most obscure movies could be viewed (and re-viewed) on demand. He takes everything he's ever seen and spins it all together into stories that may be based on other movies, sure, but at the same time are deeply personal, because he really loves those movies, and in the myopic world of movie nerds, what you love is who you are.

Alain Delon in *Le Samourai*. (Artists International/Photofest)

1

RESERVOIR DOGS: GUN CRAZY

I don't care if you want to make a buddy-cop movie starring Queen Latifah and a talking fire truck, or a portrait of a marriage in crisis influenced by the works of Eric Rohmer. If you've ever written a screenplay and sent it out into the world (or even thought about it), you've daydreamed about this scenario:

You wrote a screenplay, and a friend of a friend gave it to one of her friends. This friend of a friend of a friend is a famous actor who would be *perfect* for your movie. But this is Hollywood, and this script was passed on through highly unorthodox means, and so odds are this famous actor is just going to throw your script away. So you move on, like a grown up, and think realistically. You make plans to make the movie with your friends on a small budget ... at least that way it'll *happen*.

But the call does come. Not only does this famous actor want to be in your movie, he wants to help you raise the money for it. This famous actor's involvement takes you from a budget of $30,000 to $1.5 million, and your movie is finally getting somewhere. That movie goes on to become the talk of Sundance and a sleeper hit. A whole wave of movies aping the style of your film—starring guys who talk and act and even *dress* like the guys in your film—comes out, and your reputation as Hollywood's newest and coolest indie provocateur is established.

That's the dream, right?

Well, for a former video-store clerk and fledgling screenwriter from Torrance, California, named Quentin Tarantino, that dream was realized when Harvey Keitel called him up (yeah, yeah, their *agents* probably called each other, but it's more cinematic my way) and expressed interest in his screenplay *Reservoir Dogs*. With his characteristic self-assurance (this is a guy who often, and I mean more than a couple of times, responds to interview questions about his scripts with "Well, I'm a good writer"), Tarantino had been planning on just making the movie himself with the $30,000 he received for his screenplay *True Romance*. But his friend and producer Lawrence Bender asked him to wait just a little bit longer and gave the script to his friend, who just happened to be the aerobics instructor of Harvey Keitel's wife, Lorraine Bracco. Bender's friend then gave the script to Bracco, who gave it to Keitel, who in a fantastically lucky turn of events didn't throw away this random script given to him by his very-soon-to-be (like two-weeks soon) ex-wife. He read it, he loved it, and suddenly *Reservoir Dogs*, as we know it, was a reality.

Tarantino's inspiration for this miraculous script was an observation that heist movies, which had been around in one form or another since the silent era of filmmaking, had fallen out of fashion. So he set out to do his version of a heist movie. He borrowed the framework of Stanley Kubrick's classic *The Killing*; as he told the *Seattle Times* in 1993, "I didn't go out of my way to do a rip-off of 'The Killing,' but I did think of it as my 'Killing,' my take on that kind of heist movie." Then he added nods to the mannered films of Jean-Pierre Melville and Melville's hyperstylized devotee John Woo. After that came Woo's contemporary Ringo Lam and Lam's movie *City on Fire*, the '70s classic *The Taking of Pelham 123*, and the tough-guy legacy of New York filmmakers Abel Ferrara and Martin Scorsese. All this and more—because Tarantino is the kind of guy who remembers more about movies he saw twenty years ago than most people do about their freshman year of college—was put into the blender, and the result was a heist movie without a heist, a unique take on the crime film that would set the tone for an entire decade's worth of cinema.

THE KILLING

This complex and fractured 1956 film, which the *Chicago Reader*'s Jonathan Rosenbaum calls "arguably Stanley Kubrick's most perfectly conceived and executed film," was the movie that announced *2001: A Space Odyssey* and *A Clockwork Orange*'s Stanley Kubrick as a major filmmaking force. Stanley Kubrick's talent was such that he could make the kind of masterpiece most directors strive for their entire careers on the first try, then get bored and move on to the next genre. And indeed, after executing one of the finest heist films ever made with *The Killing*, he never worked in the genre again.

Quintessential square-jawed tough guy Sterling Hayden stars as fast-talking career criminal Johnny Clay, who is plotting an elaborate heist to rip off a racetrack, the proverbial "one last job" (does that *ever* work?) before jetting off to a tropical paradise to marry his doting girlfriend Fay (Colleen Gray). Johnny has planned every detail of the robbery down to the second, but there's one thing he can't account for: that his more amateurish cohorts do what they're told. Timid hangdog cashier George Peatty (Elisha Cook Jr.) is the first to slip up. He tells his manipulative and coldhearted wife, Sharon (Marie Windsor, a lifelong Mormon who was so often cast as a double-crossing dame or adulterous wife that she received Bibles in the mail with passages underlined condemning the "sins" she had committed onscreen), that he's gonna be rich soon and she'll love him then, by golly! Sharon, who regards George as something between dirt on her shoe and a bug to be squashed, sees her chance to rip off her despised hubby and get rich at the same time. But Sharon's not the only one with an angle. Unlike in *Reservoir Dogs*, we do actually get to see the heist in this one, and it plays out in a sequence edited together with hair-splitting precision. But that sadistic bastard, Fate, comes back to haunt Johnny in the movie's devilishly ironic punch line, which (obviously) I won't give away here but casts everything that happened before it in a new light.

The Killing was shot on a shoestring budget on an accelerated schedule; Marie Windsor claims production only lasted twenty-one days. This would be impressive for anybody, but it's downright shocking for famous control freak Stanley Kubrick. Legend has it that Kubrick intentionally drove star Shelley Duvall insane on the set of *The Shining* by berating her, belittling her, and forcing her to repeat the same hysterical lines over and over until she actually had an emotional breakdown. For one famous scene where she swings a baseball bat at Jack Nicholson, he shot 127 takes. *One hundred twenty-seven takes.* Why? So she would convincingly portray an emotionally fragile woman being tortured by a psychopath, of course. So if this same guy, the guy who once made actor Sydney Pollack do a shot where he gets up from his chair and opens a door for *two solid days*, completed an entire feature film in just twenty-one, you know his grip must have been *tight*.

THE TAKING OF PELHAM 123

Released in 1974, *The Taking of Pelham 123* is also one of the best heist movies ever made. Like *The Killing*, it's wound tighter than Jim Cramer after four espressos, and it doesn't waste a moment of its economical but highly suspenseful plot, helped along by smart writing and great editing. (Editing is absolutely essential to a good action movie. If you've ever sat through a scene where cars are exploding, bad guys are shooting, and our hero just jumped a semi on a motorcycle, but you're still bored senseless, that's at least partially the editor's fault.)

Anyway, *The Taking of Pelham 123* is caked with the gritty realism that was so popular in the '70s, shot on location in New York City. And my god, the New Yorkiness of it all...it's not every day you get a room full of overweight, loudmouthed MTA employees screaming at each other to "wait a coupla two tree minutes" in a movie. (The overwhelming '70s-ness of it all is similarly fantastic—just check out some of the fashions on the passengers of Pelham 123!)

Three men dressed in matching tweed coats, hats, glasses, and mustaches get onto a subway train (the 6, if you're interested) with large matching packages (that contain guns, duh). They are Mr. Blue (Robert Shaw), the leader and hardened professional mercenary whose last gig was leading militias in Africa; his loyal comrade-in-arms, Mr. Brown (Earl Hindman); Mr. Green (Martin Balsam), a disgraced former subway driver; and Mr. Grey (Hector Elizondo), a wild card who got kicked out of the Mob for being too sadistic. There is no Mr. Pink though. Tarantino added that one.

Our color-coded criminals hijack the train, Pelham 123, and demand a ransom for the passengers on board: "We are going to kill one passenger a minute until New York City pays us one million dollars," Mr. Blue tells the hapless employee on the other end of the radio. That hapless employee is Lieutenant Zachary Garber (Walter Matthau), head subway cop, who must figure out a way to cut through the red tape of city bureaucracy and save the passengers of Pelham 123 without letting the killers escape. Opposing him are not only the kidnappers but also his fellow transit employees, who are more concerned with making sure the trains run on time than saving the hostages. But have you ever been on a subway platform when the train is running thirty minutes late? It's not a pretty sight.

MEAN STREETS

He might be an Oscar darling now, but like Tarantino, Martin Scorsese started out as a Hollywood outsider, a kid from Manhattan's Little Italy neighborhood back when that meant something besides steep rent and cheesy tourist-trap restaurants. *Mean Streets* was actually Scorsese's third feature. He started out working under legendary B-movie producer Roger Corman, who commissioned him for the hobosploitation flick *Boxcar Bertha* (1972) after seeing his feature debut *Who's That Knocking at My Door* (1967). But after dipping his toe into the lurid world of B-movies, Scorsese wanted to make a more personal film. So he rustled up $300,000 from independent financier Jonathan Taplan (then managing roots rock group The Band) to write and direct *Mean Streets*, based on his memories of growing up in New York's claustrophobic tenements.

Scorsese cast his *Who's That* lead Harvey Keitel as Charlie, a pious and sensitive small-time crook pushed into a life of crime by his uncle, neighborhood capo Giovanni (Cesare Danova). Torn between his desire to please his uncle and his longing for a virtuous life, Charlie promises his epileptic girlfriend, Teresa (Amy

Robinson), that he'll quit the life and they'll leave the neighborhood behind forever ...just as soon as he can make some money. But Charlie's best friend and partner, Johnny Boy (a young Robert De Niro), may make even this simple dream impossible, thanks to his big mouth and short temper.

Scorsese's understanding of the rhythms of street life, his juxtaposition of grimy settings and stylish camera work, and his willingness to let the characters unfold naturally set the tone for innumerable crime films that followed—including Tarantino's. But where the two are most directly connected is in their use of pop soundtracks. *Mean Streets'* early '60s pop soundtrack sets the tone of the film so precisely it's practically a character in the movie, much like *Reservoir Dogs* and *Pulp Fiction'*s platinum-selling soundtracks. Just check out the opening scene, where Harvey Keitel wakes up from a nightmare to the sound of Ronnie Spector plaintively imploring for someone, anyone, to "Be My Baby," and it's easy to see the connection to Tarantino's signature credits sequences.

BAD LIEUTENANT

And speaking of Harvey Keitel...In the same year everybody's favorite onscreen wiseguy appeared as Mr. White in *Reservoir Dogs*, he also starred in *Bad Lieutenant* as a guy with a foul mouth, a Hoover-like appetite for drugs, and a nasty, nasty temper. The irony? In the latter, he played a cop.

Abel Ferrara is arguably the grittiest film director ever to scrape the muck of New York City off of his shoes and onto the screen, and *Bad Lieutenant* is one of his most sordid films. At the same time, it's one of his most philosophical. *Bad Lieutenant* is one of only a small handful of films rated NC-17 for graphic drug use alone, though the movie's language, violence, and (male and female) full-frontal nudity are also quite extreme. As Janet Maslin of the *New York Times* puts it, Ferrara has created "his own brand of supersleaze, in a film that would seem outrageously, unforgivably lurid if it were not also somehow perfectly sincere."

Harvey Keitel, as I mentioned, plays a cop; we never learn his name, but we learn he's a police lieutenant so desensitized to violence that he casually discusses baseball with other cops over the bodies of murder victims. On the surface a family man and a devout Catholic, underneath the Lieutenant is a simmering cauldron of anguish and rage. He smokes crack in dirty stairwells, he sexually exploits pretty young female suspects, he shoots heroin, and he compulsively gambles just to quiet the beast inside. But when he is assigned to the case of a nun brutally raped by two attackers, the Lieutenant's mask of normalcy begins to crack under the pressure of his ever-worsening bad habits. This is the role of a lifetime for Keitel, and it's difficult to overstate the intensity of his performance, whether he's watching baseball on TV or having a full-on nervous breakdown.

It should be noted that the NC-17 version of *Bad Lieutenant* is rather hard to come by and available on import only; any other version you stumble across will be heavily edited. It should also be noted that the 2009 movie *Bad Lieutenant: Port of Call New Orleans*—directed by German iconoclast Werner Herzog and starring well-known crazy person Nicholas Cage—was inspired by but is in no way a remake of this film, though it's absolutely riveting in its own demented way (just search "Nicholas Cage Bad Lieutenant Iguana Scene" on YouTube and *tell* me you don't want to see that movie!)

KING OF NEW YORK

King of New York (1990), the predecessor to *Bad Lieutenant*, is another ultraviolent character study of a fascinating but very fucked-up individual, courtesy of Abel Ferrara. Frank (Christopher Walken), an enigmatic drug kingpin unhampered by emotions or scruples in his quest for criminal dominance, is a textbook sociopath—and the hero of the film. Ferrara doesn't presume to judge Frank, a trait that Tarantino says he strives for in his own creations; as he told the *New York Times*' Lynn Hirschberg in February 2012, "I really try to not have morality be an issue at all when it comes to my characters …I let them be who they are."

As the film begins, Frank is released from prison, where he's spent half of his adult life. Reunited with his crew of Adidas-clad street pushers, he tells them that now he's living for one thing and one thing only: to make as much money as humanly possible and redistribute it to the poor (after taking his cut, of course). And how do you do that? Eliminate the competition in New York City's narcotics trade, for starters. Meanwhile, the cops are pursuing Frank more and more aggressively, and as it becomes clear he's untouchable, they decide the only way to stop a man you can't arrest is to kill him.

King of New York was (appropriately enough) shot on location in New York, the streets crackling with the energy the hip-hop scene was bringing to the city at the time. If you're into old-school rap music, black Kangol hats, and gold chains thick as your forearm, then prepare for a treat, especially when Steve Buscemi shows up dressed like a Run-DMC backup dancer as one of Frank's henchmen. Young "Larry" (though you probably know him as Lawrence) Fishburne and Giancarlo Esposito, a.k.a. Gus from *Breaking Bad*, also appear as members of Frank's multiracial crew. Frank's many monologues on "the life" are right up there with *Scarface* in the inspirational-speeches-for-gangsters department; it's not a coincidence slain rapper Notorious BIG called himself "the black Frank White" in his song "The What." For his part, Tarantino was pretty fond of the movie too: "As far as I'm concerned, *King of New York* is better than *GoodFellas*. That was about as pure a vision as you're going to imagine. I mean, that's exactly what Abel Ferrara wanted to do his entire career. It has the polish and the artistry of a pure vision and, at the same time, it's just *full on out* action."

LE SAMOURAI

> *When it comes to* Dogs, *in particular, the filmmaker that most inspired me was Jean-Pierre Melville.*
> —QUENTIN TARANTINO, *Grand Street* interview, 1994

Described alternately as the "father of the nouvelle vague" and "the garlic gangster," French film director Jean-Pierre Melville was infatuated with the stylish criminals of American film noir, to whom he paid tribute in his own movies about professional thieves and hired killers. Infused with style and self-conscious pastiche,

Melville's movies greatly influenced French New Wave directors such as Jean-Luc Godard and later on John Woo ...but more on them in a bit.

The cool thing about Melville's crooks is that they're—well—cool. Always immaculately dressed and impeccably composed, Melville's characters are true romantic outlaws who stand apart from the rest of society. And none more so than the clinically calm, cool, and collected hit man Jef in *Le Samourai* (1967). Jef is played by the immaculately pulled-together Alain Delon, who would get himself into trouble for his entanglements with the French underworld a few years later. Jef fancies himself a student of *bushido*, the way of the samurai, and while some would call all his little rituals obsessive-compulsive, he would just call them professionalism.

We really don't learn anything about Jef aside from these quirks. He's got no past and no motivation. He lives in a bare room in a run-down part of Paris and barely says a word the entire film, keeping all of his emotions and thoughts hidden (even, one might surmise, from himself). He speaks only when absolutely necessary, but that only makes it more intriguing when he calmly enters a nightclub and, after donning his trademark white killing gloves (which Melville says in his commentary are the same gloves he wears when editing a film), discreetly slips down to the manager's office to kill him.

A pretty jazz pianist working at the club witnesses the crime, but when Jef is brought in later for questioning, she says she doesn't recognize him. His alibi is airtight, so they let him go, but the shadowy group who recruited him for the job is not pleased that he was taken in. At all. So when Jef goes to meet the man who owes him money for the hit, the man instead pulls a gun on him, further complicating his already complicated dance with the police and the witness he left behind, the beautiful and similarly inscrutable young piano player. Melville's heroes are always on very lonely paths in life, and Jef Costelo is no exception; as John Woo describes them, "They are loners, doomed tragic figures, lost on their inner journey."

LE CERCLE ROUGE

Technicolor never looked as glorious as it does in *Le Cercle Rouge* (1970), a later Melville masterwork that has a rich, luscious, saturated look on the restored Criterion Collection DVD. The cinematography in this movie is incredible, and the camera often moves around the room in very long takes without cutting away, a camera technique that's also used in *Reservoir Dogs*. But if *Reservoir Dogs* is the heist movie as Shakespearean high tragedy, *Le Cercle Rouge* is the heist movie as Zen koan.

The cinematography might be the real deal, but the "quote from the Buddha" at the beginning of the film is total bullshit (or "paraphrased," if you're feeling nice) ...where have I heard that before? Oh yeah, Jules's "Bible quote" speech in *Pulp Fiction*. But like Jules's loose quotation of Ezekiel, that made-up quote is absolutely necessary, because it lets us know that the story we're about to watch is a story about fate, and no matter how far it may appear to wander (and trust me, it will wander quite far), our protagonists are destined to meet someday "in the red circle."

Corey (Alain Delon), an aristocratic thief (you can tell by his waxed mustache), gets out of jail early on good behavior on the same day that the murderer Vogel (Gian Maria Volonté) escapes from cat lover/police superintendent Mattei (André Bourvil). Vogel hides out in the trunk of Corey's car, and after escaping a police roadblock, the duo waste no time getting back to business. After robbing Corey's former boss Rico (André Ekyan), they enlist alcoholic former-cop Jansen (Yves Montand) to help them with a million-dollar jewelry heist.

A heavy cloud of inevitability hangs over *Le Cercle Rouge*, and its long, drawn-out scenes can sometimes get quite frustrating. But Corey and Vogel will not be rushed by the likes of you. Just be cool, baby, and let the movie catch you up in its current and carry you downstream. Follow the example of the actors. Unlike the Reservoir Dogs, these guys will never lose their impeccable composure. It helps that they wear trench coats and are always drinking whiskey and smoking and delivering the occasional line of carefully considered dialogue, their hats tilted at exactly the right angle. As far as philosophical meditations on fate go, you're not going to get much cooler than *Le Cercle Rouge*.

A BETTER TOMORROW

Before he conquered the Hong Kong film industry, John Woo was a nobody director of (admittedly) bad comedies. But he was always a devotee of Melville's hip killers, and in 1986 he finally got to make his (first) tribute to *Le Samourai*, *A Better Tomorrow*. The movie was a huge smash at the box office at home and abroad, changing Woo's fortunes overnight and creating a template that Asian and American action movies still copy today. The movie kicked off what became known as the "heroic bloodshed" genre, where honorable thieves (and hit men, we mustn't forget the hit men) *try* to do the right thing, opposed by a new breed of villain that cares about nothing but the almighty dollar. Since the genre allows for good guys and bad guys on both sides of the law, you'll often see cops and criminals teaming up for the greater good in these types of films.

A Better Tomorrow is a great example. It revolves around two brothers: well-meaning Sung Tse-Kit (Leslie Chung), who has just graduated from the police academy; and his elder brother Sung Tse-Ho (Ti Lung), a counterfeiter and Triad operative who works with toothpick-chomping tough guy Mark Lee (Chow Yun-Fat). Tse-Ho tries to keep his criminal activities secret from his brother, but after their father is murdered in retaliation for a crime gone wrong, the truth is exposed, and Tse-kit refuses to speak to him. After a stint in jail, Tse-ho tries to go legit and reconnect with his brother, but his ties to the gang prove hard to break.

By the time he directed *A Better Tomorrow 2* (1987), John Woo had started to develop his signature excessive visual style. Chow Yun-Fat also returned to play Mark's twin brother, Ken Lee, who dresses in trench coats too but chomps on matchsticks, not toothpicks (pretty much the only difference between them). The *A Better Tomorrow* movies revolve around the Sung brothers, but it was "Brother Mark" who really struck a chord with Hong Kong's youth. After the movies hit big, a craze for long trench coats and

Alain Delon sunglasses (endorsed by the *Le Samourai* star himself) swept Hong Kong, whose teenagers sweated it out in "Brother Mark coats" (as they're still called in Cantonese) throughout the sweltering subtropical summer. Tarantino was also quite taken with Brother Mark's style; as he said in a 1994 *Playboy* interview: "If an action movie is doing its job, you should want to dress like the hero. After I saw Chow Yun-Fat in John Woo's *A Better Tomorrow, Part II*, I immediately bought a long coat and glasses and walked around with a toothpick in my mouth."

But check this out: John Woo says he got it from Melville. He told the French cinema journal *Cahiers du Cinema* in 1996 that "I based Chow Yun-Fat's performance, his style, his look, even the way he walked on Delon in *Le Samourai*." So John Woo borrowed a style from Jean-Pierre Melville, which was then borrowed by Quentin Tarantino, whose cool gangsters in *Reservoir Dogs* were borrowed for other films...It's the circle of cinema life.

THE KILLER

In retrospect, *The Killer* (1989) has some stylistic touches—the billowing curtains, the neon lighting, the soft focus, the gratuitous slo-mo's, and all of those goddamned doves—that even Slash and his dove-obsessed compatriots in Guns N' Roses would deem excessive. It's so '80s and so over the top that you can hardly believe it was inspired by the muted tones of *Le Samourai*, but #1 Melville superfan that he is, you can bet John Woo drew from Alain Delon for this one too.

Woo pushes the melodrama to 11 in *The Killer*, starring Chow Yun-Fat as Ah Jong, a hit man who accidentally blinds nightclub singer Jennie (Sally Yeh) during a botched hit at a nightclub. The experience deeply affects Ah Jong, who starts going to the club to watch Jennie sing; eventually, inevitably, he falls in love with her. Obviously this makes him question his profession, but when he finds out that she needs a cornea transplant or she'll lose her sight forever, he accepts one more job to raise the money for her operation. Bloodshed doesn't get much more heroic than that! However, the bulk of the movie focuses on the cat-and-mouse bromance between Ah Jong and police detective Li (Danny Lee), who is in hot pursuit of this killer-for-hire but strangely drawn to him at the same time (homoerotic undertones totally intended).

The Killer received a so-so reception in Hong Kong, perhaps because it came out right after the Tiananmen Square massacre when the public had no appetite for bloodshed, even the heroic kind. But it quickly became a sleeper hit with Asian film buffs abroad (such as Tarantino), who talked it up as the totally new, totally insane future of action movies. Its legend had grown considerably by the time it screened at the 1990 Sundance film festival, which described it as: "A film concocted with nitroglycerin, which has the combined energy of *The Road Warrior*, *RoboCop*, and *The Terminator*." And thus did *The Killer* give John Woo, who later directed over-the-top action extravaganzas such as *Face/Off* and *Broken Arrow*, the Hollywood "in" that he so desperately wanted.

HARD BOILED

By 1992, John Woo was the undisputed king of Hong Kong cinema, and he couldn't wait to GTFO to Hollywood, where he would have access to bigger budgets and bigger stars. But given free rein to do whatever he wanted for as long as he wanted, he stuck around long enough to make *Hard Boiled* (1992) and amplify his signature violent style to previously unimaginable levels. Some find it repellant and some find it hilarious.

According to producer Terence Chang, *Hard Boiled*'s opening scene, a bloody shootout in a teahouse, was shot before the script was even written. Hearing that the teahouse was about to be torn down, Woo jumped on the opportunity to do his part destroying it before the wrecking ball came in. He based the entire scene around one shot: Chow Yun-Fat demonstrating his badass-itude by sliding down a banister, a gun in each hand and both of them blazing. This is our introduction to Inspector "Tequila" Yuen, a clarinet-playing Renaissance man named for his unbridled love of the aforementioned liquor.

Tequila's partner is killed in the teahouse shootout, and smelling trouble, his boss takes him off the case. But Tequila doesn't give a shit about such formalities and continues to pursue Johnny Wong (Anthony Wong), the arms dealer he blames for his partner's death. Meanwhile, undercover cop Tony (Tony Leung, who in a quintessentially Woo touch makes an origami crane for every person he's killed) is recruited into Johnny Wong's organization. Tony and Tequila are introduced when Tequila rappels down from the ceiling in a hail of bullets; luckily for Tony, he runs out of ammunition right as they point their guns at each other's heads. In the ensuing police investigation, Tequila finds out that Tony is an undercover, and so he recruits Tony to help him find Johnny Wong's arsenal. In another quintessentially Woo touch, it turns out to be located underneath a hospital morgue.

Woo had an old Coca-Cola factory turned into a hospital for the final fifty minutes of the movie, an unbelievable set piece of mayhem and carnage that Woo estimates took thirty-five days of nonstop shooting to complete. At this point *Hard Boiled* takes on the structure of a video game, as Tequila and Tony shoot their way through the hospital, level by level, trying to reach hammy, eyepatched villain Mad Dog (Kwok Choi). Meanwhile, gangsters blow up cop cars with bazookas and mow down fleeing patients with machine guns outside. Our heroes also kill everything in sight (the final body count of *Hard Boiled* is well over one hundred), but these bastards are using sick kids as human shields, so who cares, right?

Oh, one more thing—at some point Tequila stops off at the maternity ward before resuming his campaign of carnage *with a baby in one arm*. (Woo's original idea for *Hard Boiled* was about a psychopath who poisons baby food, but unsurprisingly, he had trouble financing a movie about dead babies and so rewrote it into its eventual, slightly less demented state.) Seeing no irony in the comical levels of danger he puts them in in the movie, Woo says in his Criterion Collection commentary that the babies "signify purity and hope ... we should cherish and protect these new lives." Hope getting blown off the side of a building with a bazooka. That's John Woo for you.

CITY ON FIRE

John Woo invented "heroic bloodshed," but Ringo Lam's gangster movies take an entirely different approach to the idea. Like his other movies, this gritty, intense film makes extensive use of location shooting, and the rain-soaked, neon-lit streets of Hong Kong set the tone for everything that follows. In the opening scene, a guy gets stabbed in the middle of a busy night market—a *real* night market with *real* passersby who don't seem to realize that this is all for a movie. (Lam's Hong Kong is a lawless place where mistrust of the police runs deep...you really expect him to bother with location permits?) Lam was inspired to make *City on Fire* (1987) after reading a newspaper story about a diamond heist where police surrounded the shop but didn't manage to catch any of the criminals. He began to admire the ingenuity of the thieves, which led him to ask himself, "Who is the *real* hero in Hong Kong today?"

Chow Yun-Fat stars (again!) as Ko Chow, an undercover cop who infiltrates a gang of jewelry thieves. Ko Chow is torn between his sense of duty, his guilt over betraying his new friend, Fu (Danny Lee), and pressure from his girlfriend, who just wants him to quit and get married. But Lam doesn't leave much time for Ko Chow to mope—the movie is nonstop action, going from chase scenes to shootouts to jewelry heists with barely any time to breathe. One heist a mere twenty minutes into the movie goes spectacularly wrong (like dead cops wrong), one reason that some naysayers allege that *Reservoir Dogs* "rips off" *City on Fire*. The other reasons come courtesy of a torture scene during a robbery and the last fifteen minutes of the film, where Ko Chow and the gang turn on each other while holed up in their hideout. Admittedly there are some striking similarities, but considering the films are *very* different in other respects, it's not really fair to call *Dogs* a "ripoff."

A more constructive way of looking at Ringo Lam and Quentin Tarantino is to compare the similarities in their approaches. Like Tarantino, Lam started out studying acting before he realized his talents were behind the camera. But he's also said that he prefers editing movies to shooting them, distancing himself from the characters he's created even though he bases them on elements of himself. Compare this to Tarantino, who says he "becomes" his characters while he's writing them but refuses to judge them from an ethical standpoint. They think similarly about plot too. Lam's films are also generic crime stores deconstructed to subvert the audience's expectations: "What I like to do is make up the story according to a formula, then break it down again, try to mess it up out of control," he says. That's something a Tarantino fan should certainly be able to appreciate.

THE USUAL SUSPECTS

Bryan Singer's 1995 heist film is famous for its big twist. So if sometime in the ensuing seventeen years somebody spoiled who Keyser Soze is for you, you might as well skip it, because you'll be yelling "Oh, come *on*" at the screen the entire movie. *The Usual Suspects* isn't *worthless* without the twist, but it's certainly much less fun. For that reason, I'm not going to tell you much about it, except this:

In the opening scene, a ship explodes in a harbor in San Pedro, California, killing twenty-seven men and leaving the only survivor unconscious and covered in third-degree burns. US customs agent Dave Kujan (Chazz Palminteri)'s best hope for a witness is con man "Verbal" Kint (Kevin Spacey, as the type of nondescript little man he's so good at playing), who tells most of the story in flashback. Five days ago, Kint was brought in as a suspect in an ammunitions-truck hijacking in Queens along with the rest of our titular "Usual Suspects": volatile safecracker McManus (Stephen Baldwin) and his marble-mouthed partner in crime Fenster (Benicio del Toro); irritable explosives expert Hockney (Kevin Pollak); and crooked cop Keaton (Gabriel Byrne), now trying to go straight with the help of his lawyer girlfriend. Riled up from the unexpected rendezvous with the fuzz, McManus suggests that the five of them ought to pull a job together . . .

From this straightforward premise, *The Usual Suspects* piles on layer after layer of intrigue and double-dealings before ripping it all to shreds in its final moments. You like witty dialogue? It's got witty dialogue. You like cool criminals? It's got cool criminals. You like a funky '70s soundtrack? Well, it doesn't have that, sorry. But *The Usual Suspects* does have a lot going for it…just resist the urge to go on IMDB and find out who Keyser Soze is, okay?

BE KIND, REWIND:
QUENTIN TARANTINO BEFORE HE WAS FAMOUS

Whenever you hear some crazy story about Madonna working at Dunkin' Donuts or Brad Pitt in a chicken suit outside of El Pollo Loco or whatever, you can pretty much assume it's bullshit. Like a guy who looks like Brad Pitt has to wear a chicken suit for more than a couple of days. But when it comes to Quentin Tarantino, the stories are true. He *did* work at a video store in a mini-mall—the Video Archives in Manhattan Beach, California—for most of the '80s, and many customers remember discussing movies with him at length (lucky, right?)

Before he even worked at Video Archives, Tarantino was working on a script called *Love Birds in Bondage* with his friend Scott Magill. Unfortunately the movie never really went anywhere, and what footage they had was destroyed after Magill committed suicide in 1987. More successful was *My Best Friend's Birthday*, based on a thirty-to-forty-page script Tarantino wrote about a guy who tries to do something nice for his best friend on his birthday, only to have all his plans blow up in his face. *My Best Friend's Birthday* was shot in and around the store with a cast of Video Archives employees and Tarantino's acting-class friends (Tarantino himself stars); a seventy-minute cut was completed in 1987, but a fire at the processing lab destroyed the final reel. The thirty-six minutes that survived are readily available on YouTube, and while it's an amateurish effort (what else do you expect?) it's interesting to watch Tarantino try his hand at a straight-up comedy.

And he *did* appear on an episode of *The Golden Girls* in 1988, when he was twenty-five years old. Readily available on YouTube or on DVD, it's the episode where Rose mixes up the guest list for Sofia's wedding with the Elvis fan-club meeting list, resulting in a chapel full of Elvii. Tarantino appears sitting in the back row at the wedding. You'll recognize the mug, of course, but his outfit also stands out; all the other Elvii are wearing the spangled jumpsuits of Las Vegas Elvis, but Tarantino is dressed up rockabilly-style as Sun Records Elvis. In 2003 he told *Playboy* that, thanks to syndication, the episode paid off pretty well over the years: "The job lasted two days, and what was fantastic was how much money I made...Just when I was flat broke, a check would come in for $150, then $75, then $95. I got a check the other day for 85 cents."

Tarantino quit the video store in the early '90s after his Hollywood career began to take off; in the heady days just before *Reservoir Dogs* debuted in 1992, he sold two scripts, *Natural Born Killers* (1994) and *True Romance* (1993). They both got made, but with very different results. *Natural Born Killers* was directed by the subtle-like-a-sledgehammer Oliver Stone, who also extensively rewrote the script. Tarantino hated how it came out and has publicly disowned the movie, claiming that he's never watched it all the way through. *True Romance*, on the other hand, was directed without much flair by Tony Scott, who also did *Days of Thunder* and *Top Gun*. Scott had enough sense to recognize that dialogue is key to Tarantino's stories and kept the script mostly intact. The result gives you a little more insight into who Tarantino is as person, I think, than any of his films proper. Christian Slater plays a shiftless comic-book-store employee who meets his dream girl, Alabama Whitman (Patricia Arquette), at a Sonny Chiba triple feature. It turns out she's a hooker sent by his boss to ensure he has a happy birthday, but she likes him so much they end up getting married, stealing a suitcase of coke from her pimp, and heading to Hollywood to unload it. Ah, young love...

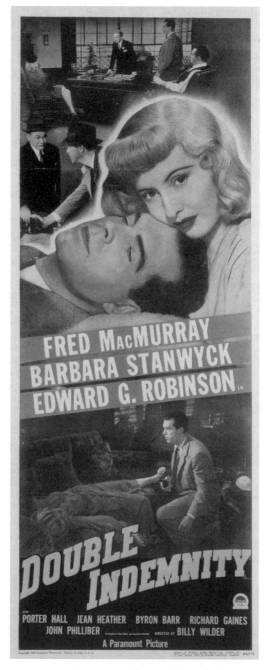

(Paramount Pictures/Photofest)

2

PULP FICTION: OUT OF THE PAST

The French loved *Pulp Fiction*.

Of course, so did pretty much everyone else. But France is a country of cinephiles, and so, Tarantino's eccentric love letter to classic crime cinema struck a special chord with the jury at the Cannes Film Festival, who gave it their highest honor, the Palme d'Or.

Highbrow legitimacy thus obtained, *Pulp Fiction* went on to gross over $200 million on an $8 million budget, rewriting the rules of what was possible for an "indie" film and bringing John Travolta's career back from the dead. For all you young'uns out there, *Pulp Fiction* was a bona fide pop phenomenon back in 1994: the soundtrack went double platinum, sparking a surf-rock revival that eventually made its way down the cultural ladder from West Coast hipsters to toothpaste commercials. You had Marge Simpson recreating the poster with a lollipop instead of a cigarette, you had Bad Ass Mother Fucker wallets lining the shelves at Spencer's Gifts, you had Royale with Cheese T-shirts and Bring Out the Gimp T-shirts and Ezekiel 25:17 T-shirts ... Actually, you know what? All of that stuff is still around now. It was just a lot more ubiquitous in 1994.

But the French, man. They were the ones who had spawned Jean-Luc Godard, the fresh new voice of a previous generation whose film *Band of Outsiders* also featured a stylish dance scene in a cafe. And they were the ones who invented the *idea* of film noir, the cinematic version of the hard-boiled detective stories that provided the spark for *Pulp Fiction*. They hadn't invented the genre—

Hollywood had done that. But the French, with their tendency toward dissecting American pop culture in far more detail than Americans ever would, looked at the crop of sexy, cynical crime pictures that was coming out of Hollywood in the 1940s and gave it a name: *noir.*

Nowadays, noir's artery-clogging innuendo is quaint to the point of being confusing. But when these movies were first unleashed upon the public, they were sordid stuff. Preachers condemned them from the pulpit, horrified hausfraus organized picket lines, and Hollywood's self-censoring Hayes Code (which would later develop into the MPAA) hovered over filmmakers' shoulders with a disapproving frown. "The Code" prohibited outright onscreen nudity, profanity, drug trafficking, interracial relationships, and "any inference of sex perversion" (among others), and in an especially condescending touch, supplemented this list of "Don'ts" with a list of "Be Carefuls" that specified that "excessive and lustful kissing, lustful embrace, suggestive postures and gestures, are not to be shown." Thus a porno shoot becomes "sitting in a Chinese chair," homosexual lovers get downgraded to loyal chauffeurs, and girls invite their male friends to pull down the shades, lock the door and have some cake...and that's all in *The Big Sleep*! Would *Double Indemnity* have included an ass-rape scene had it not been for the moralizing Mr. Hayes and his Code? Would Lauren Bacall have ODed on screen like Uma Thurman in *Pulp Fiction*? It's impossible to know, but kind of fun to think about.

When he was first developing the idea for his second feature film, Tarantino decided to take the most cliché crime plots he could think of and spin them together into an innovative three-part structure that has since been successfully applied in films such as *Amores Perros*. In this chapter, you'll meet the boxer who refuses to throw the fight, the gangster's girl who gets a little too friendly with one of her lover's employees, and a duo of wisecracking hit men for whom murder and intimidation are just another day at the office. You'll also meet pushy PIs, clueless car thieves, con artists, femme fatales, and a hooker who just can't leave her sordid past behind. They're all here, and they're all *Pulp.*

THE BIG SLEEP

The Big Sleep (1946), along with *The Maltese Falcon* (1941), is the iconic film noir, brought to you by the invisible hand of directorial god Howard Hawks. Based on the novel by mystery writer Raymond Chandler, this is the movie that introduced the iconic "Shamus," Phillip Marlowe (Humphrey Bogart), to a wide audience. What will appeal to *Pulp Fiction* fans is that like Tarantino, Hawks made dialogue a priority, and *The Big Sleep* practically combusts as the actors lob witty comebacks at each other like flaming Molotov cocktails.

The story goes like this: Marlowe is called to a meeting at the rich and important General Sternwood's (Charles Waldron) house—or rather his greenhouse, where the old man sits all day with a blanket on his lap to help relieve his aching joints. That's not the kind of problem Marlowe can help with, but Sternwood's got another problem that's right up his alley: his two daughters. Well, Vivian (Lauren Bacall), the elder sister, is married now, and he's not so worried about her, but the younger one, Carmen (Martha Vickers) ... she's wild. (She demonstrated as much by practically sticking her tongue down Marlowe's throat when they met in the foyer earlier.)

Turns out daddy dear has been receiving increasingly threatening IOUs for Carmen's gambling debts, and Marlowe's job is to get to the bottom of it. That's his job, and he's damn good at it. But she continually undermines his efforts, popping up wide-eyed and grinning in the apartment of every tough he busts in on. Marlowe's a real lady-killer most of the time, but what's a knight in shining armor to do when the princess doesn't want to be saved ... and her sister is so irresistibly seductive?

Shot during World War II (if you pay attention, you'll notice far more women than men in minor roles, as most of the men were away at war), *The Big Sleep* was shelved for two years before it was finally released. Why the delay? One, the war ended, and Warner Brothers had to rush out their patriotic propaganda films before the public lost interest. Two, after production wrapped, Bogie and Bacall became the Brangelina of their day, and producer Jack

Warner (of the Warner Brothers) insisted that more screen time of the couple be added. But this made the movie too long, and so a few key sequences (including one where Marlowe explains everything that's happened so far to the cops) were sacrificed in favor of additional star power. So if the plot gets buried under all those layers of innuendo (even writer Raymond Chandler confessed he didn't understand all the twists and turns of the story), don't sweat it, babe. Just go along for the ride.

DOUBLE INDEMNITY

Directed by another of Hollywood's all-time greats, Billy Wilder, *Double Indemnity* (1944) was kind of the *Pulp Fiction* of its day. Stop me if you've heard this one before: a movie that pushed the limits of onscreen violence but still scored big with critics and audiences alike and set the tone for its genre for a solid decade. That's what happened when *Double Indemnity* hit theater screens in 1944, foreshadowing the success of *Pulp Fiction* half a century later.

Told in flashback, *Double Indemnity* is the story of an insurance salesman (Fred MacMurray), a housewife who wants her husband dead (Barbara Stanwyck), and the insurance adjuster investigating their case (Edward G. Robinson). The title refers to a clause in the life insurance policy Walter Neff (MacMurray) sells the seductive Phyllis (Stanwyck): if her husband dies by accidental means, she stands to collect double the reward—uh, compensation—for her grief. Phyllis is the archetypal femme fatale, who, even in a (deliberately) cheap wig and tacky clothes, is able to sexually manipulate Walter into not only selling her the policy but helping her carry out the murder. But all that's just setup for the arrival of Barton Keyes (Robinson), an insurance adjuster and work friend of Walter's with a hunch about the case. Soon enough, our love birds will find that they are not as clever as they thought . . .

Double Indemnity was based on a novella by pulp writer James M. Cain, who in turn based it on a real murder trial in Queens that he had attended while working as a reporter. Wilder read the book and asked Paramount to buy the rights, which they did, although the studio considered it unfilmable thanks to that pesky Hayes

Code. But Wilder knew that "The Code" just meant you had to get creative, so he brought on *The Big Sleep* writer Raymond Chandler to help him write the screenplay. Though highly contentious (Wilder is quoted in a biography as saying, "[Chandler] was in Alcoholics Anonymous, and I think he had a tough time with me—I drove him back into drinking . . ."), the collaboration proved extremely fruitful. Chandler's hard-boiled dialogue meshed perfectly with Wilder's deft touch, and despite protests by conservative groups, *Double Indemnity* opened to generally good (if slightly shocked) reviews and great box office. Its dramatically shadowed look, for which Wilder went back to his roots in German Expressionism, set the standard for the (as yet unnamed) genre of film noir, as well as spawning a few outright rip-offs. *Single Indemnity*, anyone?

THE SET-UP

A 1949 boxing noir from the now long-shuttered RKO studios, *The Set-Up* deserves to be more famous than it is. Director Robert Wise started his career as an editor (he edited *Citizen Kane!*) and it shows; only seventy-one minutes long and unfolding in real time, *The Set-Up* is a masterpiece of taut pacing. Praised for its realism, the movie skillfully evokes the world of professional boxing—specifically, Paradise City, the kind of provincial boxing club that's the first stop for young fighters on the way up...and the last stop for aging boxers on the way down. (Ever seen that movie *The Wrestler*? This is its late '40s equivalent.)

One of the latter is over-the-hill boxer Stoker Thompson (Robert Ryan). Stoker knows that his body can't take much more abuse but is still holding out for his big comeback; after all, victory is "just once punch away," he says. He's valiantly struggling to maintain his dignity despite his perpetually worsening circumstances, but given the odds of "making it" versus just getting his brain bashed into mush, he's really a tragic figure. He doesn't give up, because he can't. We spend a good deal of the movie in the locker room with Stoker and the other boxers as they share their hopes, dreams, and fears. You really start to feel for these guys, which makes it all the more poignant when we see the crowd sadistically baying for their blood. *The Set-Up* excels at (appropriately enough) setting up the story for its devastatingly ironic ending, but before we can get there, let's start at the beginning.

Stoker is holed up in a nearby hotel, where he's feathered his love nest with his pretty young wife, Julie (Audrey Totter). Julie can't stand seeing Stoker get hurt anymore, and she pleads with him to quit. They get into an argument, and he storms out, leaving her alone in their room. Stoker arrives at the fights, certain as always that today's gonna be the day; but unbeknownst to him, his cigar-chomping, potbellied manager, Tiny, is so convinced Stoker can't win that he takes a payout for the "dive" without consulting his client. When Stoker appears to be winning three rounds into the four-round fight, Tiny tells him about the fix, but Stoker refuses to accept this final blow to his dignity and wins the fight anyway. The crowd is cheering him on, but Stoker's defiance will have some serious consequences.

Sound familiar? Elements of *The Set-Up* can clearly be seen in the "Boxer" segment of *Pulp Fiction*; but considering there's a whole subgenre of noir boxing pictures (for example, *Body and Soul* with John Garfield), and many, many of them involve a boxer who refuses to throw a fight, calling *Pulp Fiction* a "rip-off" of *The Set-Up* is like calling it a "rip-off" of *When Harry Met Sally* because they both have restaurant scenes. No, *The Set-Up* is just a great boxing noir, and one that more people should see.

KISS ME DEADLY

Dicks don't get much more dickish than Mike Hammer, and Ralph Meeker gleefully embodies this particular sadistic breed of midcentury masculinity in all of its attractive and abhorrent aspects (Men fear him! Women want him!) in *Kiss Me Deadly* (1955). This "nuclear noir" was directed with great, feverish style by Robert Aldrich and still feels innovative some sixty years later.

When the story for *Kiss Me Deadly* first crossed Aldrich's desk, he hated it. He especially hated Mike Hammer, a wildly popular sort of anti-Communist proto–Dirty Harry, whose vigilante attitude repelled the director's leftist sensibilities. But he was under contract to direct it, so he and screenwriter A. I. Bezzerides cynically reworked Mike Hammer into a parody of himself, and *Kiss Me Deadly* into a parable about nuclear war.

The backward credits sequence is a great example of the movie's uniquely off-kilter style, infused with an air of menace as if something horrible is happening just offscreen. (And in at least one scene, it is.) *Kiss Me Deadly* continually strains at the seams of '50s "respectability," implying everything even though it shows nothing. Although there's no nudity and no blood, it still has a reputation for being a sleazy, violent movie. It was condemned by moralists and dismissed as trash until decades later, a reaction that Aldrich very perceptively predicted in a *New York Herald-Tribune* piece published just before the movie hit theaters: "When *Kiss Me Deadly* reaches the theater screens of the nation, critics will probably write about and filmgoers will luridly talk of this torture scene, but at least 60 percent of what they describe will be the product of their own thinking."

We open on a lonely stretch of road somewhere outside of Los Angeles, as a barefoot woman dressed in nothing but a trench coat runs into the road, forcing a passing car to stop. This mystery woman, Christina Bailey (Chloris Leachman in her screen debut), says she just escaped from the "laughing house" and is clearly terrified. She asks the driver, Mike Hammer (who else?), to drop her off at the nearest bus stop, but before they can get to town, a car blindsides them in a spectacular crash. Mike wakes up on a filthy mattress in a strange room—just out of frame, Christina is being tortured to death, though all we can see is her feet. When Mike wakes up again, he's in the hospital, where his "assistant" (read: professional honeypot) Velda (Maxine Cooper) informs him of Christine's death. The fuzz are hot on her heels, and they swoop in to revoke Mike's PI license and warn him to keep his nose outta this one, which of course provokes the opposite reaction from the stubborn, nosy Mike.

Meeker is great in his role, as is everyone else in the cast, especially Gaby Rodgers as Gabrielle/Lily Carver, the ingénue who is not what she seems. The unfolding conspiracy revolves around a "great whatsit" in a briefcase, a plot point that is homaged in the briefcase Jules fetches for Marcellus Wallace in *Pulp Fiction*. The difference between the two is that Jules knows better than to fuck with the briefcase ... Mike Hammer, on the other hand, doesn't.

PICKUP ON SOUTH STREET

> *Unlike later practitioners described as neo- or post-, Fuller's work is at one with [its] material, not outside it. The film draws its energy from creating a world from within this pulp paradigm in all its crudity, brutality, sleaziness, and pure improbability.*
> —RICK THOMPSON, *Senses of Cinema* magazine, 2000

Pickup on South Street (1953) mines a vein of postwar paranoia similar to *Kiss Me Deadly*, delivered with the signature punch-on-the-jaw flair of Sam Fuller, America's baron of low-budget crime. Fuller started his career as a crime reporter and based his screenplays on his observations in the field, giving them a ripped-from-the-headlines immediacy that came ready-made for controversy. In his autobiography, *A Third Face*, Fuller writes that *Pickup on South Street* in particular seemed to rub people the wrong way; it was attacked in European socialist circles for being anti-Communist and in American anti-Communist circles for being pro-Communist. Fuller rather proudly adds that J. Edgar Hoover "hated" the movie and even called studio head Darryl F. Zanuck to complain about it.

Fuller exalted in the colorful language of the criminal class, and *Pickup on South Street* has some of the most delightful you're ever going to hear. Our protagonist, veteran pickpocket and "three-time loser" Skip McCoy (Richard Widmark), isn't a thief, he's a "cannon"; and he doesn't pick a lady's purse in the opening sequence, he "buzzes some moll's wallet." But he's lifted more than a couple of bucks from Candy (Jean Peters) on the subway. This perpetually bewildered anti–femme fatale was on her way to deliver an envelope as a favor for her ex-boyfriend Joey; unbeknownst to both her and Skip, the seemingly innocuous envelope is filled with nuclear secrets, for Joey is a Communist spy. He's also a selfish jerk. He blames the whole incident on Candy—

who doesn't understand why he's so upset—and makes her go out and find the guy who stole her wallet herself, because, as he says, he "can't take the risk."

So Candy goes to visit world-weary professional stool pigeon Moe (Thelma Ritter, who was nominated for an Oscar for her performance). Moe's just tired (she describes herself as "an old watch that's winding down") and wants this pushy dame out of her face, so she tells Candy the address of Skip's secret hideaway down by the Hudson River. Candy—who is perpetually trying to seduce, outwit, or otherwise put one over on men, and perpetually failing (Fuller says in his autobiography that he chose Peters because "she had Candy's bowed legs, the kind of gams you get from streetwalking")—tries her best to seduce the wallet out of Skip's hands. But thanks to a shakedown by the cops earlier that day (the cops, unlike Candy, are fully aware of Joey's identity and have been following him for months), Skip has checked out the film and knows what's on it. Calling Candy a "Red," he says he won't give up the film for less than $25,000. Candy, finally realizing the shit she's gotten herself into, bails on Joey and switches sides in the scheme. But now the Communists have been tipped off, too, and Skip and Candy are being pursued by the cops, the Feds, and the Reds.

THE NAKED KISS

Sam Fuller's *The Naked Kiss* (1964) opens with a sequence that you'll never forget: ballsy broad Kelly (Constance Towers) is beating a man with her purse. He rips off her wig, exposing her bald head, but she keeps beating him anyway until he falls to the floor, drunk and defeated. She takes seventy-five dollars from his wallet—"only what I earned," she insists—then she stands up, puts back on her wig, and begins fixing her hair as the title *The Naked Kiss* splays across the screen. And that's all before the credits start!

Two years later, Kelly has relocated to a new town, and after one last fling selling "angel foam champagne" (have you figured out she's a hooker yet?) to local lawman Captain Griff (Anthony Eisley), she has an epiphany. Seeing nothing but "the buck, the bed, and the bottle for the rest of my life," she vows to change her ways. So she gets a new job nursing sick kids, and a new boyfriend, Grant (Michael Dante), who shares her taste for Renaissance poetry and fine wine. Everything seems wonderful for a little while—even Griff, who has been not-so-subtly suggesting Kelly should just give up and go work at the cathouse across the river, gives his blessing to Kelly and Grant's engagement. But then one afternoon, Kelly drops by her fiancé's house for a surprise visit...She gets a surprise all right, and it's a terrible one. (No seriously, it's still pretty shocking fifty years later.) It's only then that we learn what a tough chick Kelly really is.

Kelly's world might not have the high-contrast lighting and deep shadows of Mike Hammer's or Philip Marlowe's, but it's definitely hard boiled. More specifically, it's pulp—noir's no-nonsense, blue-collar brother. Fuller's boldness comes not necessarily from visual style (though the camera work, particularly the editing, is often very striking) but from bold storytelling that feels audacious even when it drips with sentimentality. He shamelessly plays with our emotions by giving Kelly a new profession that's the achingly innocent opposite of her sordid former milieu: she's a nurse. (At a hospital. For crippled children.) But there's a sense of perversion festering just under the surface of *The Naked Kiss* that, for all its euphemism, just makes it even more deliciously lurid.

THE KILLERS

Also known as "Ernest Hemingway's *The Killers*," *The Killers* (1964) is a Technicolor classic of amorality starring Lee Marvin as Charlie, a proud professional hit man, and Clu Gulager as his sidekick/mentee Lee. Director Don Siegel originally intended *The Killers* to be a made-for-TV-movie, a fact that's painfully evident in the cardboard sets decorated with balsa-wood furniture and unconscionable motel-room art. But after the finished product proved too violent and morally ambiguous for Standards and Practices, the movie was hastily repackaged and released on the B-movie circuit, where those very qualities made it a cult classic.

The Killers had been adapted for the screen before—it's also a famous 1946 noir with Ava Gardner. But Siegel's version deviates from the earlier film by focusing on supercool, sharply dressed, eternally bickering professional killers Charlie and Lee, the spiritual forbears of Jules and Vincent Vega in *Pulp Fiction*. (Lee Marvin is the stone-cold Jules and Clu Gulager is the irreverent Vincent.) Both are men to be feared, Clu because he's a loose cannon and Lee because he can communicate imminent physical danger with a smile better than most people can screaming at the top of their lungs. (And if he leans in to whisper in your ear? You'll probably wet your pants.) Also bringing a *Pulp Fiction*–like flair to the proceedings is the comical violence of Charlie and Lee's techniques. In one hilarious scene, Charlie and Lee aggressively shake down a mechanic for information, launching him into an extended, emotional confession; the camera zooms out from his tear-covered face to reveal Charlie and Lee idly fiddling with their guns, bored stiff. Hey, it's a living.

Here's another everyday incident in the life of a hit man: Lee and Charlie muscle their way into a school for the blind, wearing their sunglasses the entire time in cruel mockery of the children's disability, and coolly start terrorizing the plump, middle-aged receptionist for the location of teacher Jerry Nichols, a.k.a. Johnny North (John Cassavetes). After accidentally pointing their guns at a classroom full of little blind children, they finally find him and finish the job. Here's the weird part: even though he's been tipped off that they were coming, Johnny doesn't put up much of a fight—no fight at all, as a matter of fact—a detail that's bugging Charlie as he and Lee are relaxing and having a drink on the next express train out of town. He wants to know why they got $25,000—$15,000 more than usual—for the hit, and why North just stood there and waited for them to kill him. So over Lee's objections, Charlie decides to take a break from murdering people for a few days and get to the bottom of this mystery.

Most of *The Killers* is told in flashback, *Citizen Kane*–style; turns out that Johnny North was a race-car driver and, more specifically, a race-car driver who made the mistake of falling for the wrong girl. That "wrong girl" is the flirtatious Sheila (Angie Dickinson, re-imagining the femme fatale as emotionally vacant arm candy), mistress of gangster Jack Browning (Ronald Reagan [!!], cast against type as a bad guy). Johnny's love for Sheila is so all-consuming that it keeps him up at night and thus makes him crash his car; while he's recovering at the hospital, his buddy/mechanic Earl informs him that Sheila has been two-timing him with a man who would kill him without hesitation. Betrayed and frightened, Johnny attempts to cut off all contact, but Sheila won't take no for an answer. And as we know from *Pulp Fiction*, when a hood gets involved with the boss's lady, it never turns out well for the hood.

POINT BLANK

The existential crime-thriller *Point Blank* (1967) throws you off-kilter starting with its delirious opening-credits sequence. Told partially in flashback, the sequence shows how Walker (Lee Marvin) was double-crossed and left for dead by Mal Reese (John Vernon), a "friend" who stole Walker's wife, Lynne (Sharon Acker), in the bargain. But it's cool. Walker manages, somehow, to recover from his bullet wound alone on the concrete floor of an abandoned jail cell, then swims back to San Francisco, emerging just as a passing tour-boat operator explains that "no one" could survive the swim across the bay.

Walker might be superhuman, but Lynne isn't, and when he finally finds her in Los Angeles, she's a pill-addled mess who's haunted by the role she played in Walker's betrayal. He considers killing her; before he can make up his mind, she does it for him by ODing on her meds. Walker mourns his wife's passing for, like, two minutes (Walker has no use for sentimentality), before moving on to rough up a used-car salesman with "Outfit" connections. The terrified middleman tells him Reese has been hanging around Lynne's sister Chris (Angie Dickinson), so with Chris's help, Walker begins his campaign to systematically take down Reese and the entire corporatized Mob that he works for.

It's a clichéd story, but what makes *Point Blank* unique is the lack of emotion in Walker's actions. He certainly has reason to harbor a grudge, but as Walker makes very clear to anyone that asks, he's not looking for revenge. He just wants his money. It's really not that much money ($93,000 to be exact), not enough to justify all those deaths, but still Walker presses on. And *Point Blank* refuses to show us the "real Walker" underneath his terrifyingly placid surface, to reassure us that it's okay, he's like us after all. Because Walker is nothing like us.

Much of *Point Blank* unfolds like a dream, with highly stylized action and muffled sounds that make you feel like you're underwater. As Lynne tells Walker as she dozes off into a chemical stupor, "You ought to kill me. I can't sleep, I keep taking pills ... I keep dreaming ... I keep thinking about you ... how good it must be, being dead ... is it?" Also like a dream, the movie's structure is intentionally disconcerting: it lulls you into complacency with long, slow sequences and then peppers them with sudden, brutal acts of violence. The narrative is fractured, quite literally, in a shot where Marvin and Dickinson are reflected in a cracked mirror—Walker is kind of a cracked mirror himself. (Some even interpret the entire film as a dream, a revenge fantasy that plays out in Walker's mind as he lies dying on the cold concrete floor of Alcatraz.) The then-contemporary mod look oozes from every frame, and *Point Blank* is also a really cool time capsule of mid-'60s Los Angeles scenery and style, with the coldness of Walker's character reflected in the impersonal landscapes of concrete, glass, and steel.

Point Blank was a passion project for Lee Marvin, who acted as the de facto codirector of the movie, making stylistic suggestions (including the color-coordinated set design) and holding rehearsals at his house. Director John Boorman says in his DVD commentary that they met while Marvin was in London shooting *The Dirty Dozen* (chapter 7); they hit it off and talked about the novel *The Hunter*, which they had both read and both hated ... except for the main character. A guy named Walker. So when he got back to LA, Marvin pulled some strings and managed to get total creative control over the project—control he would later have to exercise when skittish studio heads suggested extensive cuts to the film. At first, the suits' fears seemed to be justified when *Point Blank* failed at the box office. But over time, its stature has grown considerably, proving once again that when Lee Marvin speaks, you don't ask questions. You just obey.

BREATHLESS

Back before Jean-Luc Godard became an elder statesman of cinema, or even the voice of a generation, he was just the director of *Breathless* (1960). It's not an exaggeration to say *Breathless* was "revolutionary"—it helped launch a whole new style of filmmaking called the French New Wave (or the "nouvelle vague" if you're being a snob) that brought a whole new energy and sense of playfulness to world cinema.

One of *Breathless*'s key innovations, and one that is essential to the later development of Tarantino's style, is its celebration of so-called "low" culture. Godard's heroes are obsessed with American movies, talk endlessly about American movies, and take their behavior cues from American movies; movies are even woven into the fabric of the movie itself. Like Tarantino, on one level Godard's doing it consciously, but on another he's just being true to his own experiences and those of his pop-culture fixated peers. There were no video stores when Godard was young, but before he became a film director, he did work as a film critic, a job that allowed him to soak in the cinematic clichés he would later reinterpret for his own films.

Michel (Jean-Paul Belmondo) is a small-time car thief who wears a fedora in tribute to his hero, Humphrey Bogart. Michel is also a cocky, arrogant know-it-all and a committed skirt chaser. So when he meets Patricia (Jean Seberg), a willowy, pretty American with a chic Mia Farrow hairdo (five years before Mia Farrow had it, thankyouverymuch), he's instantly reeled in. After all, it's his two obsessions, America and pretty girls, together in the flesh at last.

Patricia is bored. She's trying to work her way up at the *New York Herald-Tribune*, but this being the early '60s, they give her such exciting, important tasks as fetching coffee and selling newspapers on the street. So she invites Michel and the trouble that follows him into her life. Michel tells her he's a car thief; no problem. He impulsively killed a cop that pulled him over, he says; it kind of turns her on. Michel plans on collecting some debts before he leaves Paris, but as he hangs around waiting and flirting with Patricia, what he doesn't realize is that the noose is already around his neck, and it's getting tighter by the moment.

The 1983 remake of *Breathless*, starring Richard Gere and Valérie Kaprisky, reverses the premise so we get an American hood and a French exchange student in Los Angeles, but beyond that, it sticks to the plot of the original. What it does add are pop-culture references that will be right up any Tarantino fan's alley; as Tarantino himself said about it, "Here's a movie that indulges completely all my obsessions—comic books, rockabilly music, and movies."

BAND OF OUTSIDERS

All of the women in *Pulp Fiction* are, in some way, a tribute (conscious or unconscious) to Anna Karina, Jean-Luc Godard's wife and muse of *Band of Outsiders* (1964). It's all there, embodied in her oversize sweaters, gorgeous wide eyes, and the subtle ingenue smile that plays on her lips. It's also there in cool (at least, they think they're cool) criminals Franz (Sami Frey) and Arthur (Claude Brasseur). Though these guys are positively bush league compared to Jules and Vincent, they spend their time leading up to the big (at least, they think it's big) crime hanging out, smoking cigarettes, reading newspaper articles aloud, recounting the plots of movies, telling jokes, and just generally shooting the shit. Plus, it's got an ultracool synchronized dance scene where our characters do the Madison in a half-empty cafe! Still not convinced? How about this, smart guy: Tarantino's production company, A Band Apart, is named after this movie's French title, *Bande à Parte*. The cultural references are different, because they come from a different time and place, but the irreverent, stylish spirit they share makes *Band of Outsiders* and *Pulp Fiction* cinematic kin.

Band of Outsiders tells, with frequent digressions, the tale of how Franz and Arthur meet Odile (Karina), appropriately enough at an English class, and sweet talk her into joining them in their life of small-time crime. The trio starts planning a robbery, using Odile as their accomplice in robbing her own suburban house. But as it turns out, seeing lots of crime movies isn't enough to make you good at crime. However, the crime itself is incidental; *Band of Outsiders* is more about what happens in between that fateful meeting and its fateful consequences.

Godard uses quite a few innovative techniques in *Band of Outsiders*, such as "breaking the fourth wall" (letting the actors acknowledge that they're in a movie by directly addressing the camera) and the "minute of silence" (a sequence where Franz, Arthur, and Odile decide to observe a "minute of silence"; as soon as it is decided, all the ambient noise drops off and the soundtrack goes completely silent ... for thirty-six seconds). The film comes by its off-the-cuff quality honestly; Godard shot *Band of Outsiders* in only twenty-five days, letting the actors make up much of the dialogue as they went along. The only thing in the movie that was rehearsed was the famous (and easily Google-able, by the way) dance scene, which Godard claims they practiced for two or three weeks—almost as long as it took to shoot the entire rest of the movie.

Later in his career, Godard took a sharp turn toward the experimental with an emphasis on leftist agitprop. But thankfully, in *Band of Outsiders* he eschews politics and applies his cinematic trickery sparingly, creating his most accessible, and arguably most charming, movie in the process.

THE GRIFTERS

Like *Pulp Fiction*, *The Grifters* (1990) takes the conventions of the crime films of the past and updates them for the modern era. Like *Pulp Fiction*, it's set firmly in contemporary (i.e., early 1990s) Los Angeles. But unlike *Pulp Fiction*, it doesn't have a cool pop soundtrack; in fact, the generic Danny Elfman-ish score is one of the weakest things about it. And unlike *Pulp*, it doesn't seek to reinvent the genre. *The Grifters* is simply a loving homage—a light, quirky, snappy riff on a novel by tough-guy writer Jim Thompson.

Directed by Stephen Frears under the patronage of Martin

Scorsese, *The Grifters* is tense and full of surprises. The dialogue recalls the witty repartee of classic noir ("You talk the talk," Roy tells Myra, the highest compliment this movie can give) without relying on the cheesy slang, the "dolls" and "dames" and "cannons" and "operators." But the coolest thing about *The Grifters* is that it shows you the techniques, mind games, and sleight-of-hand tricks employed by working grifters, or con men. And the way it all comes together makes you feel like you're peeking behind the curtain at a magic show.

The story revolves around our three leads: First there's Roy Dillon (John Cusack), a small-time grifter who works the "change scam" on bartenders in between dazzling schmucks out of their petty cash. Then we have Lilly (Anjelica Houston), his estranged mother, currently under the employ of a powerful mobster. Lilly's scam is working the ponies, manipulating the odds so track owners never have to pay out too much to some jerk who got lucky on a long shot. Finally there's Myra (Annette Bening), Roy's girlfriend, who, unbeknownst to him, hustles her way through life selling fake diamonds and screwing her landlord for the rent.

Lilly arrives at Roy's apartment in LA unannounced one afternoon, throwing him completely off balance; you know immediately that there is something wrong with their relationship when she coyly greets him with a "Long time no see" and a kiss on the lips. Lilly had Roy, her only child, when she was just fourteen years old, and a distinct incestuous current runs through their relationship. But despite this (or maybe because of it), they haven't spoken in eight years and can barely contain their hatred for each other. ("Get off the grift, Roy. You haven't got the stomach for it," Lilly spits at her son when he tells her that he's a "salesman.") "Displeased" would be an understatement for Lilly's response when she meets her son's main squeeze, and being the domineering, venom-spitting viper she is, she sets out to regain the top spot in Roy's affections. Anjelica Houston was nominated for an Academy Award for her role in *The Grifters*, and she does a great job giving depth to Lilly, who in a lesser film would have become a cartoon villainess.

AMORES PERROS

You can't really call *Amores Perros* (2000) a *Pulp Fiction* ripoff, since its gritty neorealist style doesn't borrow much from Tarantino's slick sensibility. So when people refer to director Alejandro González Iñárritu's knockout debut as "The Mexican *Pulp Fiction*," what they're referring to is its distinct three-part structure. Like *Pulp Fiction*, *Amores Perros* is composed of three stories, and they all come together at one pivotal moment—in this case, a dramatic car crash that is repeated several times throughout the movie.

Amores Perros's first story stars a young Gael Garcia Bernal as Octavio, an unemployed youth hopelessly smitten with his brother Ramiro (Marco Pérez)'s wife Susana (Vanessa Bauche). Susana and Ramiro have a tense relationship after having been forced into a shotgun marriage; Ramiro works as a cashier by day and a stickup man by night, but doesn't bring any money home to his family. Meanwhile, Octavio has started entering the family dog into dogfights, and as it turns out, the dog's a natural, winning a lot of fights and making a lot of money. (There has been some controversy surrounding the dogfighting scenes in this movie, which can be quite upsetting if you come across them unawares; Iñárritu insists that no dogs were hurt and the Mexican ASPCA was on set during all of the dogfighting scenes.) Octavio and Susana eventually begin a desperate and passionate affair, but Susana's true feelings remain complicated and mysterious...

The second storyline takes us to a much higher strata of Mexican society for the story of magazine publisher Daniel (Álvaro Guerrero) and supermodel Valeria (Goya Toledo). Their story interacts with Octavio's when Valeria's car violently collides with his; we pick up as the badly injured Valeria returns to the new apartment she and Daniel share. She is depressed and worried that her looks, and therefore her modeling career, are ruined, so Daniel gets her a dog to keep her company. But this just causes more friction when the dog gets stuck underneath the floorboards of the apartment and won't (or can't) come out. Stuck in the prison of the apartment, Valeria grows more and more unstable...

The third storyline follows a bagman on the streets of Mexico

City: El Chivo (The Goat) (Emilio Echevarría). He appears to be a hobo pushing a shopping cart through the streets with a gaggle of stray dogs. Okay, he is, but he's more than that too. A former schoolteacher, he got involved with a guerilla movement twenty years ago and now works as a hit man. He's out on a job when the car crash that affects our other characters occurs, and he's interrupted before he can make the kill. In the ensuing chaos, he rescues Octavio's critically injured dog and takes it home with him, oblivious to its violent nature …

All three stories in *Amores Perros* (loosely translated as "Love's a bitch") are about dogs, yes, but underneath that they're about people betrayed by those they love, like a dog who rolls over and shows its belly when kicked. It's a deftly done and impressive work, especially considering it's a debut feature, and it's well worth your time.

THE DOG-EARED MENACE:
PULP FICTION FOR *PULP FICTION* FANS

If you like *Pulp Fiction*, then why not read yourself some real Pulp Fiction? There are still a few yellowing paperbacks lying around from the golden era of pulp publishing, though they grow rarer and rarer every year. Instead, check out the gigantic anthology *The Black Lizard Big Book of Black Mask Stories* for hard-boiled classics from the pulp magazine that initially inspired Tarantino. *Hip Pocket Sleaze* by John Harrison (Headpress Books) is also an excellent overview that can help point you towards your particular cup o' sleaze; do the lesbian pulp novels of Ann Bannon turn you on, or are you more of a *Satan* magazine type of guy (or gal)? Either way, *Hip Pocket Sleaze* has you covered.

Then there are the undisputed masters of detective fiction, the ones who wrote the books (and sometimes the screenplays too) for many of the films in this chapter. Dashiell Hammett—former private eye, veteran of two wars, and raging alcoholic—was the "dean" of the hard-boiled school of crime fiction; his 1929 novel *Red Harvest* is an American classic, though he also created the beloved characters Sam Spade (the private eye from *The Maltese Falcon*) and Nick and Nora Charles (The *Thin Man* movies). His fellow faculty included Raymond Chandler, who wrote eight Phillip Marlowe novels in his lifetime (seven and a half, actually—one was finished after his death): *Farewell, My Lovely*; *The Little Sister*; and *The Long Goodbye* are all considered classics. And then there's James M. Cain, who began his career as a journalist and imbued his stories with facts pulled from real cases; his novels *The Postman Always Rings Twice*, *Double Indemnity*, and *Mildred Pierce* have all been adapted for the screen multiple times.

After these godfathers of the genre came a nastier breed of pulp writers, chief among them Jim Thompson. Thompson, who hit his stride in the early- to mid-'50s, is most famous for a pair of novels that provide a chilling first-person glimpse into the minds of two seriously psychotic individuals (and coincidentally, small-town Texas sheriffs): *The Killer Inside Me* and *Pop. 1280*. Though he was ahead of his time (none of his books were in print when he died in 1977), Jim Thompson is now one of the highest-regarded pulp writers for his unrelentingly bleak outlook on humanity and his flair for the surreal.

Speaking of bleak, let's talk about Hubert Selby Jr., author of *Last Exit to Brooklyn* and *Requiem for a Dream*—hands down two of the most harrowing books you will ever read in your life. Told in a dense stream-of-consciousness style, they descend into the absolute lowest depths of society, a feverish hell of junkies with gangrenous arms and hookers gang-raped and left on the street to die. Over the years, Selby's blunt realism has made several of his books cult classics. A contemporary of Selby's who also dealt in harsh truths was Iceberg Slim, a former pimp whose autobiographical novel *Pimp*, published in 1969, told it like it was from someone who had been there.

Lesser known but just as deserving are crime writers such as Steve Fisher, who wrote the thrilling Hollywood noir *I Wake Up Screaming*; Horace McCoy, who used a dance marathon as a metaphor for existential despair in *They Shoot Horses, Don't They?*; Charles Willeford, who tells the tale of a car salesman turned movie mogul in the excellent

The Woman Chaser; and Donald E. Westlake (a.k.a. Richard Stark), who was unjustly obscure for many years but whose series of "Parker" books (which also inspired *Point Blank*) have gained tremendous popularity in recent years, thanks to a series of graphic-novel adaptations from artist Darwyn Cooke.

And then there's Elmore Leonard, "The Dickens of Detroit" and reigning king of crime fiction, whose crackling dialogue and zippy storylines have formed the basis for everything from the FX series *Justified* to a little movie called *Jackie Brown* ...

Pam Grier is Foxy Brown. (American International Pictures/Photofest)

3

JACKIE BROWN: BIG BAD MAMA

By the time Jackie Brown hit theaters in 1997, Quentin the Wunderkind, the boy genius who could do no wrong, had done some wrong. Sure, *Pulp Fiction* was an instant classic praised everywhere from *USA Today* to *Cahiers du Cinema*, but after that, what do you have? *Four Rooms*, that's what.

So abandoning the collaborative projects that were getting him nowhere, he returned to the well for his next project. He returned to the work of Elmore Leonard, whose books he had first fallen in love with as a kid and whose cinephile hit men and eloquent thieves had inspired an early success, *True Romance*. As Tarantino told the UK's *Telegraph* newspaper in 2010:

"He was probably the biggest influence on my life. I have been reading Leonard since I was 14 and got caught stealing his novel *The Switch* from K-Mart. I got in huge trouble. I was grounded all summer long. But I was so pissed off that I didn't manage to get the book that two days later I went back and stole it proper."

So for his next movie, Tarantino chose to adapt the Elmore Leonard novel *Rum Punch*, changing the emphasis of the story to world-weary flight attendant Jackie Brown and infusing it with the spirit of another one of his childhood obsessions—blaxploitation.

Okay, let's back up for a second. "Blaxploitation" is the word for a cycle of movies that flourished on the American independent film scene from about 1971 to 1977. "White flight" was in full swing during this period, and demand for the bland Hollywood fare that catered to conservative middle-class white people was leaving the inner cities along with them. But the elegant movie palaces that had been erected during the early days of cinema were still there, only now it was people of color that were filling them. And those same people of color were hungry for representations of themselves on the big screen, inspired by the Black Power philosophy that was in vogue at the time. In a way, it was a simple case of supply and demand.

Though many of the people who helped create it don't like the word, blaxploitation represented a seismic shift in the way African Americans were represented in popular culture. Before blaxploitation, the conventional wisdom in Hollywood was that movies featuring black faces wouldn't "draw." But when independently produced movies such as *Sweet Sweetback's Baadasssss Song* and *Shaft* started to outgross their own pictures, producers began to sit up and take notice. And without blaxploitation, there would be no Denzel Washington, no Will Smith, no Jamie Foxx, no Samuel L. Jackson ... or at least, not as we know them today. Before movies such as *Black Caesar* and *Coffy*, there were no black action heroes for little kids to look up to, especially not female ones. The people who looked like them had always played servants and sidekicks. But blaxploitation made them heroes.

Sure, blaxploitation movies are usually violent, and often full of gratuitous nudity. It was the '70s! But they're also a vibrant and infectiously funky time capsule. Blaxploitation is an attitude as much as it is a period in cinema history: it's loud patterned shirts with plaid bellbottoms; it's Afros and dashikis; it's funky bass lines; it's jive talk; it's dignity and self-reliance; it's the unwavering belief that Black is beautiful, and its appeal cuts across all boundaries of time, place, and race.

Tarantino grew up in Los Angeles (the South Bay beachfront community of Torrance, California, to be exact) during the heyday of blaxploitation, and he would blow off school to go to the movies and rapturously take in all the blaxploitation movies that played there. So for his big return to form, he cast one of the genre's greats, actress Pam Grier (who was in need of a comeback herself), as his

Jackie Brown: a strong, mature woman with the will to survive no matter what. And it was perfect.

COFFY

She'll cream you!

Coffy (1973) established Pam Grier as the shotgun-toting "Queen of Blaxploitation" and spawned a legion of imitators, many of them also starring Pam Grier. But according to director Jack Hill, *Coffy* was brewed out of spite. In his DVD commentary for the film, Hill explains that one afternoon, he was called into the office of a producer at American International Pictures, where he was told that he was to do a "black-woman revenge movie." Turns out that the writers of a movie called *Cleopatra Jones* had met with AIP about buying the rights to their script, only to turn around and sell it to Warner Brothers instead. So Hill was tasked with making a movie that would outperform *Cleopatra Jones* (with more violence and more nudity, naturally) on a smaller budget. And despite the odds, he did.

Hill immediately thought of actress Pam Grier, whom he had previously worked with on a couple of Women in Prison pictures. Grier was a natural, whose relaxed and confident screen presence made her stand out among her sometimes-stiff peers. Deciding that she had exactly the right take-no-prisoners attitude, he began writing the part of Flower Child Coffin, a.k.a. Coffy, especially for her. Hill wrote Coffy as a superhero with no superpowers, a tough-minded woman who uses her "wits, wiles, and sexuality" as her weapons ... along with the occasional switchblade or shotgun, of course. (Grier was already an old pro with weapons by the time she made *Coffy*; there were no black stunt women who looked even remotely like her at the time, so she performed her own stunts out of necessity. Not only that—Hill says that she came to set excited and full of ideas, even dreaming up the famous scene where Coffy hides razor blades in her Afro!)

Grier announces her presence in a major way in *Coffy*'s opening scene, where she poses as a junkie who will do anything (or anyone) to get her fix, then blows away the drug dealer who takes her home with her shotgun. Coffy is a surgery nurse who hates drug dealers with a passion, especially after her little sister ODs on smack *at age eleven*. Enough is enough, and so Coffy sets out on her own personal quest for revenge, using her connections with the junkies and hookers she's treated at the hospital for information. Working her way up the food chain, she uses a ridiculous Jamaican accent to talk her way in with the outrageous King George, a pimp with narcotics connections. But Coffy is Coffy, and even when she's supposed to be working undercover, she can't help but assert herself, pulling a gun on a client who humiliates her with racist remarks and starting a ridiculous cat fight at one of King George's parties with the aforementioned Afro full of razor blades. And you better believe she gets to the bottom of it in the end, because honey, Pam Grier always gets her man.

FOXY BROWN

> *She's brown sugar and spice, but if you don't treat her nice,*
> *she'll put you on ice!*

After the runaway success of *Coffy*, Jack Hill and Pam Grier reunited for a sequel, *Foxy Brown* (1974). Like Coffy, Foxy Brown is a tough and resourceful woman with a personal vendetta against the pushers and the dealers. See, Foxy's brother Link (Antonio Fargas) is a drug dealer whose life is going down the tubes, the exact opposite of her undercover-FBI-agent boyfriend Michael (Terry Carter). Michael has been undergoing facial reconstruction surgery to protect himself from the criminals he's busted, but Foxy's no-good brother rats him out to Miss Katherine (Kathryn Loder), the local madam/dealer/scum-of-all-trades. Miss Katherine sends her right-hand man Steve Elias (Peter Brown) to kill Michael, and Foxy quickly puts two and two together and makes her brother give up the motherfuckers who did this to her man. Like Coffy, Foxy's greatest asset is her ability to be tough and sexy in equal measure, and so she has no trouble bluffing her way into a job at the abrasive Ms. Katherine's cathouse, where she goes through a lot of hell before finally getting her revenge.

Foxy Brown isn't quite as good as *Coffy*, though when you've got Pam spouting Jack Hill's signature sassy dialogue, you really can't go wrong. Here's an example: when a hooker, played by legendary stunt woman Jeannie Epper, tells Foxy not to mess with her 'cause she's got a black belt in karate, an unimpressed Foxy replies "—and I got my black belt in barstools!" before smashing one over her head.

T. N. T. JACKSON

She'll put you in traction.

Jeannie Bell, recipient of the dubious Ebony Fist Award (former Roger Corman employee Joe Dante claims the award was made up to obscure Bell's lack of a martial arts background) stars in the kung fu/blaxploitation hybrid *T. N. T. Jackson* (1974). The movie comes courtesy of good old Cirio Santiago, a prolific director of '70s Filipino exploitation who thought he was making high art when he was really making high camp. The execution of the movie leaves something to be desired, but as they say, it's got heart—it's too cheesy to be sleazy (despite the questionable naked fight scene) and too earnest not to love.

When we first see Jeannie Bell, she's wandering around "Chinatown" (in what city the movie never really makes clear, but it's somewhere in the Philippines) with her suitcase in hand. Within minutes of her arrival, she's challenged to a street fight by a large gang of karate experts, because, well, that's what happens to everybody in Chinatown, right? Jeannie's fish-out-of-water story arc, combined with her calm self-assurance, is definitely reminiscent of The Bride's Asian training sequences in *Kill Bill*, but let's be clear: Jeannie Bell didn't learn martial arts for the role like Uma Thurman did. She's no martial arts expert. She's not even that good at pretending to be a martial arts expert...although her stunt double isn't bad. What she is, is a tough broad with a nasty attitude who takes no shit from no one ("The Name's Diana Jackson ... that's T. N. T. to you," she tells anyone who asks). However, she does accept help from Joe (Chiquito), a local bar owner and martial arts expert who assures her he is "only Chinese in body," whatever that means.

T. N. T. is looking for her missing brother, who also happened to be a student of Joe's. With his help, she worms her way into the local heroin racket using Charlie (Stan Shaw), the black right-hand man of the Man who (say it with me now) wants to offer her work as a hooker, as her in. But when the shit hits the fan, T. N. T. needs no help from man or woman, gangster or cop. *T. N. T. Jackson* is undoubtedly silly and occasionally incompetent, but there's never a dull moment, and it would be worth checking out just for the climatic "light switch" scene that was homaged in *Jackie Brown*.

SWEET SWEETBACK'S BAADASSSSS SONG

Rated X by an all-white jury!

When it comes to blaxploitation, *Sweet Sweetback's Baadasssss Song* (1971) is the movie that started it all...although maybe not to the extent that director Melvin Van Peebles will have you believe. If you ask him, every single blaxploitation movie ever made was a direct response to *Sweet Sweetback*, but that's not accounting for *Shaft* (1971), which was already in production by the time *Sweet Sweetback* hit theaters, and arguably was more influential on the aesthetics of the genre. See, *Shaft* is an action movie, like most blaxploitation movies, and *Sweet Sweetback* is more of a Black Power art film that combines ghetto realism with shooting techniques inspired by the French New Wave. But *Shaft* or no *Shaft*, *Sweet Sweetback* was first, and it was revolutionary, and it wore its X rating as a badge of honor.

An early example of an "indie" film as we know them today, *Sweet Sweetback* is a movie that no producer would touch but all of them tried to imitate. Van Peebles famously wrote, starred in, directed, scored (the music was performed by a then-unknown Earth, Wind & Fire), and produced *Sweet Sweetback* by himself, at least partially because he couldn't afford other people to do those things for him. Plus he, uhm, did his own stunts—Van Peebles claims that he contracted gonorrhea while filming one of the movie's many supposedly unsimulated sex scenes, a condition for which he applied to the Directors Guild of America for worker's compensation. It was granted.

Van Peebles got that DGA card during an earlier incarnation as an in-house director for Columbia Pictures, for whom he directed the 1970 feature *Watermelon Man*. He says that working within the system was a terrible experience, especially dealing with censorship-happy executives, so he asked himself: "Since what I want is The Man's foot out of our collective asses, why not make a film about a brother getting The Man's foot out of his own ass?" Obviously, no studio would finance a movie about that—who's The Man more than a movie producer, after all?—and so Van Peebles secured independent financing (Bill Cosby famously gave $50,000) and shot the film completely independently with a predominantly nonwhite crew.

Sweet Sweetback is completely in-your-face real, starting with its opening sequence: a scruffy little street kid is taken in by a group of prostitutes, and the next thing you know, this skinny kid (played by the director's own son, Mario, who can't be any older than ten) is stripping butt-naked and mounting one of the ho's, who dubs him "Sweet Sweetback" on account of his extraordinary organ. Fast-forward to the present day, where he's still making his living with that fantastic dong as a performer in a live sex show. The cops have been sniffing around, looking for low-hanging fruit (pun intended), and they arrest Sweet Sweetback on trumped-up charges. But the cops can't even wait until they get back to the station to chase down and beat up a young black militant, and when Sweet Sweetback comes to the boy's aid, he is forced to go on the run. Sweet Sweetback's people (he's down with all kinds of marginal groups— blacks, Mexicans, gays, hippies) help him escape LA, and he has a pseudomystical experience crossing the desert with his wang as his only weapon. (Is it just me, or is it kind of egotistical to write a movie about a guy with a magic penis and then cast yourself?)

If you're interested in the story behind the making of *Sweet Sweetback*, check out *Baadasssss, or How to Get the Man's Foot Outta Your Ass* (2003) a pseudodocumentary homage to Marvin by his son Mario Van Peebles. Mario plays his father during the making of *Sweet Sweetback* and gives some historical context about how revolutionary the movie really was.

SHAFT

The Mob wanted Harlem back. They got Shaft ...up to here!

Shaft (1971), as I just mentioned, came out hot on the heels of *Sweet Sweetback's Baadasssss Song*, and you might be surprised to learn that this unapologetic exploitation movie was directed by Gordon Parks, a pioneering black photographer who was the first African American to work for *Life* magazine and the cofounder of *Essence*. Shaft (Richard Roundtree) is a swaggering dude in a cool black leather coat who works as a private detective (the baddest of all professions, ya dig?) in New York City. Shaft is hired by a black crime boss to find his kidnapped daughter in the midst of an uptown/downtown gang war. The movie was phenomenally successful, earning what *Time* magazine called an "extraordinary" $13 million in US theaters on a budget of $500,000. Shaft's financial success had casting directors all over town looking for the next black action hero; the effects of this change are still being felt in Hollywood today.

Of course you know the soundtrack by Isaac Hayes: just turn to the person next to you and say "he's a bad motha—" and I guarantee you way more people will know the next line (answer: "Shut yo mouth") than have actually seen the movie. Hayes's iconic "Theme from Shaft" won an Oscar and a Grammy and has been parodied in everything from *The Simpsons* to the BBC sitcom *Father Ted*; combined with its position at the vanguard of the movement, these factors have made *Shaft* both the most famous blaxploitation movie and one of the most celebrated.

SUPERFLY

Never a dude like this one! He's got a plan to stick it to The Man!

And then we have *Superfly* (1972), directed by *Shaft* director Gordon Parks's son Gordon Parks Jr., another box-office phenomenon that signaled the arrival of the blaxploitation generation. Ron O'Neal, he of the outrageous wardrobe, luxurious mane, and even more luxurious mustache, stars as Priest, an independent coke dealer who lives a life of fur-lined early-'70s luxury—hot bitches! Champagne! Flashy cars! More bitches! Color TVs! But Priest longs to escape the game, and so he sets up his biggest deal ever in hopes of cashing out and splitting town in his custom 1971 Cadillac Eldorado. But the Mob doesn't have a retirement policy, and if Priest wants to leave the life, it's going to cost him his life.

Made in a transitional moment after the narcotics trade had started to flourish in inner-city America but before the crack epidemic devastated entire communities, *Superfly* is an unabashed ode to the drug-dealing lifestyle. It represented a break from the old Mob (and Mob movie) code that considered drug dealing "beneath" them, and played a major role in making the "pusher" the folk hero he is today. Buoying the movie's glamorous depiction of drug dealing was the hit soundtrack by soul singer Curtis Mayfield, who declared in the song "Pusherman": I'm your doctor when in need/ Have some coke, have some weed…I'm your pusherman . . ."

Despite any lingering moral ambiguity, mainstream critics embraced *Superfly* back in 1972, and audiences still embrace it today. Harry Knowles of *Ain't It Cool News* is a fan, saying in his review of an Alamo Drafthouse revival screening that "A film like this makes you feel cool to be a human." Recommendations don't get much stronger than that!

THE MACK

There's a new kind of hero on the streets!

The Mack (1973) is a fascinating window into the black street culture of the early '70s, a kaleidoscope of Afros, loud prints, sunglasses worn at night, big wads of cash, three-card monte, craps, and jive. Ah, jive. Armchair sociologists will get quite a kick out of hearing its unique proto–hip hop speech patterns coming out of the mouths of pimps at the barbershop, at the player's ball, on the streets, and in their cars. You just don't hear people talking like they do in *The Mack* anymore, except when they're trying to parody things like *The Mack*. And *The Mack* does come off sometimes as the stuff of parody, partially because so many have parodied it, but also because of some truly weird sequences that will make you howl with laughter. Like what? Like a planetarium scene where a pimp hypnotizes his bitches with a galactic light show that doubles as a ho-ing motivational speech. Like that.

This master of astrological mind control's name is Goldie (Max Julien), an ex-junkie from a "broken home" as they called it in those days. Goldie just got out of jail after being put away by corrupt, racist cops Hank (Don Gordon) and Jed (William Watson), who will continue to harass him throughout the movie. His first stop after getting out of the joint is a pool hall, where elder hood The Blind Man (Paul Harris) welcomes Goldie home by declaring that Goldie doesn't have to risk his ass stealing TVs anymore, because he is going to introduce him to the mackin' game. Goldie is reluctant at first, but he turns out to be a natural who quickly rises to the top of the game with his "soft as velvet, hard as steel" approach to his bitches. Goldie even wins the 1973 Pimp of the Year award at the annual Player's Ball! (A pimp softball tournament and the annual Player's Ball? You spoil us, movie.) But when you're at the top, man, you know suckas are gonna try to take you down...And yeah, that is *the* Richard Pryor in a supporting role as Goldie's main man, though this was at the height of his coke-binge days and you can tell he's a little, uh, scattered.

Like *Superfly*, not only does *The Mack* refuse to judge Goldie, it comes down firmly on the pro-pimping side, portraying Goldie's violent outbursts and emotional manipulation of his "bitches" as a necessary evil. This unease at the heart of the movie is best illustrated in a scene where Goldie rolls up on a ghetto street corner in his fancy car and flashy suit; he greets the mob of curious kids who gather round his ride with dollar bills, patting them on the head and telling them, "Stay in school. Don't be like me." There are several points throughout the movie where you think Goldie's on the cusp of changing his ways, that he's going to stop profiting on the backs of others (literally), only to have him behave more like a heartless criminal than ever in the next scene. It's highly morally ambiguous, but a lot of that depends on your view of pimps going in. Goldie might not be above smacking around the highly vulnerable women in his employ, but hey ...he bought his mom a house, I guess.

In terms of direction, character development, and script, *The Mack* is definitely a cut above, but that probably is just because it lacks the Ed Wood-esque attention to detail that hinders some other blaxploitation films. And although it doesn't loom as large as *Shaft* in the popular consciousness, *The Mack* was the highest-grossing "black" movie of the period, and its devoted fanbase includes Tarantino, who named it one of his Top 20 "Grindhouse" movies of all time.

BLACK CAESAR

> *Hail Caesar, Godfather of Harlem...the cat with the .45-caliber claws!*

Ladies and gentlemen, Fred "The Hammer" Williamson is in the building. This former football star, future King Cobra spokesman, and October 1973 Playgirl Man of the Month appeared on network sitcoms such as *Julia* and *M.A.S.H.*, and even an episode of *Star Trek*, but they call him the "original gangsta" thanks to his blaxploitation roles. Williamson was inspired to quit the NFL for the slightly less dangerous field of acting by fellow jock-turned-thespian Jim Brown (who costarred with Williamson in *Three the Hard Way*, about a fiendish plot to infect the US water supply with a serum deadly only to African Americans). Fred Williamson is, to put it bluntly, the man, and he'll be popping up over and over again for his roles in the original *Inglorious Bastards* (chapter 7), *From Dusk Till Dawn*, and his series of blaxploitation/Western hybrids (chapter 8), but *Black Caesar* (1973) might just be the performance of his career.

Black Caesar updates the story of *Scarface* (the 1932 original, not the one with Al Pacino, although it does draw from the same source) and moves it to the streets of Harlem. Williamson stars as Tommy Gibbs, a.k.a. Black Caesar, a boy whose destiny is decided from the moment he is assaulted by a cop on the take while working as a shoeshine boy. As a result, Tommy has a massive chip on his shoulder against the cops and the Mafia (*Black Caesar* is as much a Mobsploitation movie as a blaxploitation movie), and he won't take no for an answer in his quest for power. Driven by rage and resentment, Tommy quickly rises to the top of the black syndicate; this gives him not only the clout to muscle his way in with the bigoted Sicilian mob but the private army to declare war on them. Williamson is great as the outwardly tough but inwardly wounded Tommy, and a climactic scene where he relives a painful racist incident from his past while confronting a Mafia don is a real knockout. Plus, the movie has a fantastic, funky James Brown soundtrack (which I personally prefer over the *Shaft* or *Superfly* soundtracks), as is to be expected for blaxploitation.

Director Larry Cohen (along with Jack Hill, one of the great B-movie directors of the '70s) was famous for his laissez-faire attitude and rarely, if ever, asked permission before location shoots. In the documentary *American Grindhouse*, Williamson recalls his days shooting *Black Caesar* with a laugh, saying: "I learned a lot from Larry Cohen. I learned how to shoot without permits, [and] how to steal shots." AIP, the studio that produced *Black Caesar*, asked Cohen for a sequel, but he and Williamson were living on opposite coasts at the time. However, Cohen used his famous ingenuity to work out a plan: he shot *Hell up in Harlem* (1973) on weekends, using stand-ins for Williamson on location in New York and flying out to Los Angeles, where Williamson was shooting another movie, to film close-ups.

ACROSS 110TH STREET

If you steal $300,000 from the mob, it's not robbery. It's suicide.

You'll instantly recognize the theme song from *Across 110th Street* (1972)—it was a hit for singer/songwriter Bobby Womack back when the movie came out, and then in 1997, Quentin Tarantino chose it as the theme song for *Jackie Brown*. *Across 110th Street* is a gritty, realistic cops-and-robbers movie shot on the trash-covered streets of Harlem with a predominately black cast, but many critics argue that it's unfair to call it "blaxploitation." See, *Across 110th Street* isn't primarily about racial issues, and it doesn't celebrate outlandish fashion or pimp culture or any of those other blaxploitation gimmicks. It's just a crime story that happens to be set in Harlem. And if the black element is incidental to the story, you can't really call that blaxploitation, right?

The plot concerns the hunt for two guys who dress up like cops and stick up the drop for a Mafia numbers game, stealing $300,000 and taking out a few crooked cops in the process. Afterward, not only is Mob enforcer Nick D'Salvio (Anthony Franciosa) after them, so are police detective Frank Mattelli (Anthony Quinn) and his partner, Detective Lieutenant Pope (Yaphet Kotto). Mattelli and Pope are as different as can be—Mattelli is older, white, and on the take, and Pope is young, black, and on the straight and narrow. Both are great, especially in their scenes together, and reason enough to make *Across 110th Street* a sleeper classic.

DETROIT 9000

Visit the murder capital of the world—where the honkies are the minority!

Across 110th Street is a serious crime drama that gets lumped in with blaxploitation. *Detroit 9000* (1973), on the other hand, might aspire to such gravitas, but that's just not its place in the world. What it is, is a scrappy little cop movie full of naive charm and funky blaxploitation attitude, and baby, there ain't nothin' wrong with that. *Detroit 9000* was shot on location (appropriately enough) in Detroit, capturing the city as it was beginning to oxidize from a titan of industry to a rust-belt relic. So the acting isn't *Raging Bull*, so what? It's the spirit of the thing that counts, and the spirit of *Detroit 9000* is the kind of thing that makes you happy to be alive.

The crème de la crème of Detroit's black elite has come to fete congressman Aubrey Hale Clayton (Rudy Challenger), but before the ink on the checks can dry, the party is interrupted by stick-up men in black ski masks. They relieve the partygoers of $400,000 worth of jewelry and cash before splitting, leaving the guests to cower on the floor to threats blaring over the loudspeaker from a cassette tape. As you might expect, these wealthy and influential people are quite upset about the incident, so the cops put two detectives on the case: world-weary white detective Danny Bassett (Alex Rocco, who later costarred in *The Godfather*) and suave, intelligent black cop Sergeant Jesse Williams (Hari Rhodes). They're polar opposites: Danny has been ground down into a cynical, hunched-over little man by years of watching his peers get promoted while he's busting skulls on the streets, and Jesse is not only a perfect physical specimen ("whoever doesn't believe black is beautiful never saw my big hunk'a man meat," as his girlfriend puts it), he's well educated, charismatic, honorable, and clean cut—he was an all-American jock in high school, for Christ's sake.

It's kinda like *Lethal Weapon* with more loaded racial rhetoric, and the racial element is loaded with rocket fuel in this movie. *Detroit 9000* goes there, over and over again, from throwaway lines such as "No wonder the honkies think we're oversexed" to a vicious, bigoted rant from a feeble old woman in a wheelchair, but it saves special vitriol for its portrayal of the deeply hypocritical nature of institutional racism. It's a stupefying reminder that the '70s really were a different time. And you can thank Tarantino for that—he rescued this fascinating time capsule from obscurity and released it on his sadly short-lived Rolling Thunder Pictures video label, still the best release *Detroit 9000* has seen on VHS or DVD.

BLACK DYNAMITE

He's super bad. He's outta sight. He's...

There were blaxploitation parodies before *Black Dynamite* (2009)— *I'm Gonna Git You Sucka*, for example, or *Pootie Tang*—but Michael Jai White's homage to all things hip, cool, and funky is my favorite, because it not only nails both the style and tropes of blaxploitation perfectly, it's really fucking funny to boot. It differs from other blaxploitation parodies in that it doesn't try to update the genre, but throws itself wholeheartedly into the super-fly '70s—funky fashions, cinematic growing pains, and all.

White & Co. clearly have a lot of affection for the genre, and they pack the movie full of visual shoutouts to different movies, *Kill Bill* style. Every blaxploitation trope there is shows up at one point—the pimps (all famous comedians, such as Arsenio Hall and Cedric the Entertainer), the Black Panthers (including a hilarious orphanage scene that's clearly a takeoff of *Coffy*), and The Man (just wait and see what happens with Pat Nixon). Another great touch are all the little details such as intentional continuity errors, haphazard editing, and dangling boom mics, a nod to the fact that classic blaxploitation filmmakers often had more enthusiasm than technical skill.

So anyway, Black Dynamite starts his quest to bring down the Man, who is flooding the streets with *drugs* and decimating the *community* and the *children* after his brother Jimmy (Baron Vaughn) is killed while working undercover for the CIA. To aid him in his quest, and to get the attention of gloriously Afroed honey Gloria (Salli Richardson), he teams up with a Black Power group; but just as Black Dynamite has cleaned up the streets seemingly for good, Anaconda Malt Liquor comes on the scene, and ooooo it is mean! So Black Dynamite has to bring down the Man controlling the Man whose ass he already kicked. That's where the karate comes in…

Black Dynamite is full of laugh-out-loud funny lines, such as the scene where Black Dynamite and the boys simultaneously deconstruct the Man's diabolical plan and invent chicken and waffles and lines like these: "Dr. Wu! Your knowledge of scientific biological transmogrification is only outmatched by your zest for kung fu treachery!"

Kung fu treachery, you guys. Kung fu treachery.

OUT OF SIGHT

Opposites attract.

Another entry into the Elmore Leonard movie canon, *Out of Sight* (1998), comes courtesy of Stephen Soderbergh, the other poster boy for the '90s indie-movie revolution. Soderbergh won the Cannes Palme D'Or award in 1990 for his first feature, *Sex, Lies, and Videotape*, which went on to receive an Oscar nomination for Best Original Screenplay and put Soderbergh on a Tarantino-esque rocket to fame. After his breakthrough, however, Soderbergh directed a series of low-budget box office disappointments, and so the pressure was on for this, his big "return to form" based on an Elmore Leonard novel. Luckily for Soderbergh, *Out of Sight* delivered with critics and audiences, and Soderbergh went to win that Oscar for *Traffic* (2000) and direct, among others, the *Ocean's Eleven* movies, *The Informant!* (2009), *The Girlfriend Experience* (2009), *Contagion* (2011), *Haywire* (2012), and the male-stripper dramedy *Magic Mike* (2012).

George Clooney stars at the cusp of his transition from TV heartthrob into Hollywood leading man as Jack Foley, a suave professional thief and confidence man who lands in jail when his getaway car fails to start after a bank robbery. He's in the process of breaking out of the joint when he meets federal marshal Karen Sisco (Jennifer Lopez...I know, I know, but don't worry, she's actually good in this one), who is pointing a shotgun at his face. But Jack and his partner, Buddy (Ving Rhames), who has come to pick him up, get the jump on Karen; Buddy scoops her up and tosses her in the trunk with Jack, where even in these close quarters, the chemistry is immediate.

Thus begins the mating dance of Foley and Sisco, playing cops and robbers as a form of wild, pheromone-driven jungle flirtation. Their "opposites attract" romance is intertwined with the story of a million-dollar diamond heist Buddy and Richie are planning with Snoopy (Don Cheadle), a former boxer and acquaintance from the joint with ambitions of striking Scarface-style fear into his minions' hearts. *Out of Sight* boasts a skillfully interwoven nonlinear storyline that flashes back and forth between Foley and Buddy's prison days and the present; a tough female lead worthy of a Pam Grier movie in Karen Sisco; and of course, all the thrilling, witty wordplay that Elmore Leonard is famous for.

TEN SOULFUL ALBUMS FROM BLAXPLOITATION
SOUNDTRACK ARTISTS
(...AND ONE THAT NEVER QUITE MADE IT)

ISAAC HAYES (*Shaft, Shaft's Big Score, Truck Turner*),
    Hot Buttered Soul

CURTIS MAYFIELD (*Superfly*), *Curtis*

MARVIN GAYE (*Trouble Man*), *What's Going On*

JAMES BROWN (*Black Caesar*), *Make It Funky/*
    The Big Payback, 1971–1975

ROY AYERS (*Coffy*), *Vibrations*

BOBBY WOMACK (*Across 110th Street*), *Understanding*

HERBIE HANCOCK (*The Spook Who Sat by the Door*),
    Headhunters

EARTH, WIND & FIRE (*Sweet Sweetback's Baadasssss Song*),
    That's the Way of the World

DONNY HATHAWAY (*Come Back, Charleston Blue*), *Live!*

SOLOMON BURKE (*Hammer*), *Keep the Magic Working:*
    The Original, 1955–1961

THE FINAL SOLUTION, *Brotherman: Music from the Motion Picture*

ROBERT RODRIGUEZ

Tarantino's best filmmaking buddy is Austin, Texas–based writer/director Robert Rodriguez, a patron saint of the '90s indie movement known as "the one-man film crew." His legend began with 1992's *El Mariachi*, the "$7,000 movie" partially financed with money Rodriguez made as a human lab rat in pharmaceutical experiments at the University of Texas. Of course, Rodriguez was an old pro by the time *El Mariachi* came along; he estimates he made about forty movies on his dad's VHS camcorder before he graduated high school, and says, "Every filmmaker has thirty bad movies in him, and the sooner you get 'em out, the better off you are."

Rodriguez met Tarantino at the Toronto Film Festival, where they sat on a panel about violence in the movies (of course). The two were kindred spirits (in a 2008 interview, Tarantino recalled talking to Rodriguez for over an hour and a half in the lobby of their hotel), and before they left, they promised that they would work together sometime.

The first opportunity came with Rodriguez's 1995 movie *Desperado*, where Tarantino makes a cameo as a manic drunk guy who tells bartender Cheech Marin a joke about pissing all over a bar (sounds about right). Their next collaboration was the disastrous 1995 anthology movie *Four Rooms*, where they teamed up with fellow indie auteurs Alison Anders (*Gas, Food, Lodging*) and Alexandre Rockwell (*In the Soup*) for what was supposed to be the cinematic equivalent of Crosby, Stills, Nash & Young but ended up more like Freebass. Rodriguez's segment about two kids up to no good when their parents go out for the evening is cute and foreshadows his later *Spy Kids* movies, but Tarantino's is positively cringeworthy, as Tarantino himself stars alongside Bruce Willis as the regrettably fast-talking embodiment of mid-'90s Hollywood excess. Tim Roth does his best to tie it all together as the goofy bellhop, but he's trying way too hard, as is everyone else involved with this mercifully quickly forgotten production.

They teamed up again in 1996 for *From Dusk Till Dawn*, written by Tarantino and directed by Rodriguez, and thankfully much better than *Four Rooms*. Tarantino costars alongside George Clooney as one half of the sibling criminal team Richie and Seth Gecko, on the lam and racing toward the border after sex offender, homicidal maniac, and general sick fuck Richie breaks professional killer Seth out of the joint. Seth and Richard's trail of carnage leads them to a roadside motel, where they kidnap a disillusioned preacher (Harvey Keitel) and his kids—innocent bible-study-type daughter, Kate (Juliette Lewis in a bit of stunt casting), and withdrawn adopted Chinese son, Scott (Ernest Liu)—and use them as cover to get across the Mexican border. These odd bedfellows then head to Seth and Richie's rendezvous point, the Titty Twister, where after Richie licks whiskey off of gorgeous stripper Satanico Pandemonium (Salma Hayek)'s foot (one of the privileges of writing the screenplay, I suppose), the film shifts suddenly and dramatically from an action comedy to a vampire horror bloodbath. (Tarantino's acting roles have been somewhat . . . controversial, but he's actually pretty good in *From Dusk Till Dawn*.)

Now I may be biased, but the first half, the "Tarantino half," plays better than the "Rodriguez half." The script is packed with Tarantino's trademark hilarious hard-boiled lines, such as when Seth tells Pete Bottoms (future Academy Award nominee John Hawkes), the lone employee of Benny's World of Liquor, that he better get rid of the sheriff quick or "you can change the name of this place to Benny's World of Blood." The second half has some awesome cameos (Tom Savini and Fred Williamson, who delivers the obligatory Vietnam monologue) and the clever over-the-top weaponry that Rodriguez is famous for, such as super soakers filled with holy water and a hydraulic wooden stake. But while Robert Rodriguez is great at crazy ideas, he's not as good at suspense, so by around the third wave of vampire battles, *From Dusk Till Dawn* runs out of steam.

Since then, they've continued to collaborate, as Tarantino guest directed a scene in *Sin City* (2004), as well as, obviously, *Grindhouse* (2007)—and with *Sin City 2* on the horizon, we can look forward to a lot more from the cinematic team of Tarantino and Rodriguez.

Sonny Chiba in *The Streetfighter*. (New Line Cinema/Photofest)

4

KILLBILL: VOLUME 1:
THE BLOOD-SPATTERED BRIDE

Kill Bill (2003–2004) **is the ultimate movie lover's movie:** the point where the reverential, referential aspects of Tarantino's work reach their greatest heights. Whereas in the past he was simply adapting his favorite movie clichés into his own offbeat style, he treats *Kill Bill* almost like a rap album, "sampling" musical cues and specific shots from his favorite exploitation movies to give in-the-know fans a sort of cinematic fist bump right through the movie screen. It's the work of a passionate filmmaker who is also a passionate film fan. As Peter Rainer said in his review in *New York* magazine: "There is no ironic overlay in Tarantino's movies, no 'commenting' on the pop schlock he's replicating. He simply wants to remake in his own way the kinds of movies he's always loved, and he's about as uncynical as a movie geek can be."

The *Kill Bill* movies take place in a "movie universe" where all of Tarantino's favorite characters also live; as he said in a 2003 *Playboy* interview, "This is a movie that knows it's a movie." *Pulp Fiction* and *Reservoir Dogs* take place in a world that's like Los Angeles but a little different (what Tarantino refers to as the "realer than real"), but *Kill Bill* is another layer removed from our reality, and in the "movie universe," our laws do not apply. Everything Tarantino's done belongs to either the "realer than real" or the "movie" universes (except for *Jackie Brown*, which belongs to its own Elmore Leonard universe). Within these universes, the characters can move around and hypothetically meet each other; for instance, the girl gang from *Death Proof* could hang out with Jules from *Pulp Fiction*, because they live in the same Tarantino-verse. However, none of them could meet Beatrix or Bill, because their Tarantino-verse is on a whole other plane. But they *could* go see *Kill Bill* in a movie theater in their universe, and they'd probably love it.

Another cool thing about *Kill Bill* is that you don't have to pick up on all the references to enjoy it, but it certainly doesn't hurt. It holds up exceedingly well to repeated viewings, and even if you've seen *Kill Bill* before, I suggest that you watch all the movies in the next two chapters and then go back and watch both volumes again. You'll pick up on layers of detail that weren't there before. Just as *Kill Bill* is split into two volumes, there are too many influences to discuss in one chapter, so I've divided them into two. First we explore the Japanese action cinema whose influence is more clearly seen in *Kill Bill: Volume 1*. So fasten your seat belts and stow your samurai swords in an upright locked position, because we're on our way to Tokyo...

THE LONE WOLF AND CUB SERIES

There's something about samurai movies from the '70s that invokes the aesthetics of comic books, and the Lone Wolf and Cub series is the penultimate achievement in that ultraviolent, cartoonish style. The Lone Wolf and Cub movies are based on a hugely popular manga series by Kazuo Koike that was brought to the US in the '80s with covers by Frank Miller and Bill Sienkiewicz; you may also have heard the story in the graphic novel/movie *Road to Perdition* or at the beginning of *Liquid Swords.** Well, technically that's *Shogun Assassin*—a lot of people know the assassin Lone Wolf and his son Cub from that film, a spliced-together highlights reel of the first two Lone Wolf and Cub movies that was released in the US and UK with insane dubbing from Lamont Johnson and Sandra Bernhard. (You may recall that this is the movie B.B. wants to watch when she's finally reunited with Beatrix at the end of *Kill Bill: Volume 2*.)

In Koike's world, lady ninjas jump clear out of their kimonos and run backwards; baby carts come equipped with spears and machine

---

* You know, *Liquid Swords*, right? The GZA album. *Really?* Oh, that's one of the rules, man. Yeah. If you like Quentin Tarantino, you *have* to be down with the Wu.

KILL BILL: VOLUME 1

guns; and everyone and everything (including shoji screens, sand dunes, and statues of the Buddha) bleeds. The Lone Wolf and Cub movies are incredibly violent, but they're also so hyperstylized that the two pretty much cancel each other out. Rivers of blood spray from the arteries of Lone Wolf's many victims like they're attached to pressurized hoses (and they are). Sounds gory, but the thing is, the blood is *bright orange*. And sometimes people don't bleed blood at all in Lone Wolf and Cub...one guy "bleeds" dust as he's giving his dying soliloquy! In Lone Wolf and Cub movies, people never die instantly—well, *important* people, anyway. Nobody ever stops to give a speech in one of the many House of Blue Leaves–style battles where Lone Wolf slaughters an entire army single-handedly. But if it's an important duel, one we've been building toward the entire movie, then there's always plenty of time to give a speech on what an honor it is to be killed by the great Lone Wolf before you draw your last breath.

Japanese screen star Tomisaburo Wakayama stars as Ogami Itto, a.k.a. Lone Wolf. In his youth, Wakayama was a famed martial artist known for playing screen heavies, but by the time the first Lone Wolf and Cub movie came out in 1972, it looked as though he had been hitting the rice bowl pretty hard. Being big is never a problem when you're trying to be intimidating, however, and in a way, it just makes Lone Wolf even cooler when you see him outdraw and outfight men twice as fit as he is. His Cub is the adorable Akihiro Tomikawa (just wait till you see him jumping up and down and clapping those cute fat baby hands) who began acting at age four and retired at age six when the film series wrapped.

The first movie, *Sword of Vengeance* (1972), largely sets up the back story for the series, and so it's got more talk and less gonzo violence than the rest. Here's the basics, courtesy of *Shogun Assassin*:

> When I was little, my father was famous. He was the greatest Samurai in the empire, and he was the Shogun's decapitator. He cut off the heads of 131 lords for the Shogun...My father would come home to mother, and when he had seen her, he would forget about the killings.

He wasn't scared of the Shogun, but the Shogun was scared of him. Maybe that was the problem...Then, one night the Shogun sent his ninja spies to our house. They were supposed to kill my father, but they didn't. That was the night everything changed...

You really ought to watch *Sword of Vengeance* though. It makes the subsequent adventures so much richer, and it's got some great scenes of its own, like the one where Lone Wolf sets a ball and a sword in front of his infant son and tells him, "I know you can't understand me, but you must choose. If you choose the sword, you will join me. If you choose the ball, you will join your mother [implication: in hell]." Cub chooses the sword, and so he becomes a demon like his father. But from the expression on Wakayama's face, you know that if he had chosen the ball, Lone Wolf would have followed through.

The second movie, *Baby Cart at the River Styx* (1972), is my personal favorite. Now we're really in the swing of Lone Wolf and Cub's adventures as traveling assassins-for-hire, and in this volume, they do battle with a clan of lady ninjas hired by Lone Wolf's mortal enemies, the villainous Yagyu Shadow-Clan, all leading up to an awesome battle in a massive bank of sand dunes. Ogami Itto comes to the aid of an imperiled prostitute and gets tortured for his trouble in the third movie, *Baby Cart to Hades* (1972), which also has an exceptionally good duel at the end; O-Yuki, a female assassin, briefly joins up with the father-son assassination team in the fourth movie, *Baby Cart in Peril* (1973); in the fifth, *Baby Cart in the Land of Demons* (1973), they fight the ferocious Masked Clansmen of Kuroda while on a job. And the last Lone Wolf and Cub movie, *White Heaven in Hell* (1974), features Lone Wolf slaughtering ski ninjas (!) during what the trailer proudly proclaims is the "largest snow field massacre ever filmed"! And of course, that diabolical Yagyu Shadow-Clan—led by Lord Restudo, or as I like to call him, He-of-the-White-Caterpillar-Eyebrows (Oki Minoru)—is right on his heels, cackling maniacally, the entire time.

LADY SNOWBLOOD

A beautiful woman in a white silk kimono staggers through the gently falling snow. Finally she collapses, and a puddle forms around her delicate body as the white powder is soaked through with crimson blood. The camera pans up as this fallen warrior bleeds to death in the winter cold, and the cathartic strains of "The Flower of Carnage" begin to swell on the soundtrack...

Okay, so: that's the climactic scene of *Kill Bill: Volume 1*, right?

Right. But it's *also* the end of the 1973 samurai revenge epic *Lady Snowblood: Blizzard from the Underworld*.

The female assassin O-Yuki, better known as Lady Snowblood, was another comic creation of Kazuo Koike, and in adapting it for the screen, director Toshiya Fujita took a story that was equal parts bloodbath and soft-core porn (oh, Koike, you incorrigible smut hound) and took out the soft-core porn, transforming it into the tragic and surprisingly serious, but still violently lurid, tale of a woman who was born from death and trained to kill.

Our story begins long ago in Meiji-era (late nineteenth through early twentieth century) Japan. A newborn baby's cries echo off of the stone walls of a women's prison. The mother is on the brink of death, but just before she succumbs, she holds the baby in her arms and names her Yuki. She implores her infant daughter to remember her poor mother and her father and brother, for whose vengeance Yuki must sacrifice her life. Yuki (family name Kashima)'s father and brother were murdered nearly a year ago by a gang of four assassins (introduced in a dramatic low-angle shot directly homaged in *Kill Bill*) for the crime of looking like government tax collectors. This felonious foursome then kidnapped Yuki's mother and subjected her to a living hell of rape and torture; one day she snapped and killed her captor, which is how she landed in the jail where she now lies dying. One of the villains who wronged Yuki's family died that day, but the other three remain unfinished business.

And that's just the back story! Yuki is raised by a stern and demanding Buddhist priest named Dokai (Ko Nishimura), who teaches her the way of the sword. Dokai tells Yuki that she is a "child of the underworld," a demon in human skin who can never

71

know love. Her sole purpose in life is to exact bloody vengeance for the family she can never meet. Under this cruel discipline, Yuki grows up to become the supernaturally beautiful Meiko Kaji, who can communicate more with her big, cold eyes than most actors can with pages' worth of dialogue. Since women were officially forbidden from carrying swords in the Meiji era, Yuki carries a thin blade hidden in her umbrella, which Kaji wields beautifully in all of her fighting scenes. Kaji was the uncontested queen of Japanese exploitation in the '70s, and her formidable rep as an action heroine reaches its peak in *Lady Snowblood*.

Like *Kill Bill: Volume 1*, *Lady Snowblood* gets more and more intensely violent as Yuki checks her enemies off of her kill list, culminating in an intensely bloody showdown at a Western-style fancy dress ball. O-ren Ishii's sartorial sense and back story will definitely have a familiar ring once you've seen *Lady Snowblood*, though the inspiration is not as literal as some of Tarantino's detractors like to suggest. But with its breathtaking murder set pieces, elegant visual sense, and one of the most badass lady assassins in movie history, *Lady Snowblood* is an absolute must-see for fans of *Kill Bill*.

HANZO THE RAZOR SERIES

Like Ogami Itto and Yuki Kashima, Hanzo "The Razor" Itami sprang from the twisted imagination of manga artist Kazuo Koike. And if you think the flying ninjas of Lone Wolf and Cub or the balletic bloodspray of *Lady Snowblood* were over the top, you ain't seen nothing yet.

Hanzo is Koike's version of the "cowboy cop" who plays by his own rules ... y'know, like Bruce Willis in *Die Hard* or Gary Busey in *Bulletproof.* Hanzo's mission is to root out corruption wherever it may hide in the capital city of Edo (modern-day Tokyo), and if he had a badge, he'd be turning it in every fifteen minutes. Sadly, Hanzo doesn't have a badge, but what he does have is a secret weapon. No, he's not a master swordsman, and no, he's not superhumanly strong, though he does have an exceptional ability to withstand torture. Ladies and gentlemen, Hanzo the Razor has weaponized his penis.

Hanzo has been gifted with the titular Sword of Justice, a member of such exceptional size and toughness that he is obligated—nay, divinely ordained—to screw the truth out of the wanton women of Edo. Every scheming chamberlain and corrupt official has a mistress, right? There's a sequence at the beginning of the first film, *Sword of Justice* (1972), where Hanzo, uhm, tempers his sword by pouring boiling water on it and plunging it into a bag of rice. He then places it on an anvil and begins smacking it with a wooden mallet as a funky '70s porn groove plays in the background. It's ludicrous B-movie surrealism at its absolute best.

Compared to Lone Wolf and Cub or *Lady Snowblood*, which retain some element of seriousness even at their most excessive, Hanzo the Razor is the funniest of the three. It's also the most unapologetically sleazy—there's an undercurrent (hell, it's more of an *over*current) of sexual assault that runs through the entire series. None of Hanzo's "informers" take his sword willingly at first, though this being an exploitation movie, they go from screaming and struggling to moaning with delight and babbling all of their lovers' secrets in about ten seconds flat. (Hey, there was no such thing as political correctness in 1972, least of all in Japan.) Luckily, Hanzo the Razor is so cartoonish that you can't even take the icky rape bit all that seriously. Speaking of cartoonish, did I mention that Hanzo's house is tricked out, James Bond–style, with hidden panels full of spring-loaded weapons that he shows off to his lady companions during a postconfession soak?

And if you think it couldn't get any more absurd, check this out: Shintaro Katsu, the actor who played Hanzo, was the real-life brother of fellow action star Tomisaburo Wakayama (a.k.a. Lone Wolf). Not only that, but Shintaro also played the blind swordsman Zatoichi. Now if you're not familiar, the character of Zatoichi is an icon of samurai cinema and one of its most beloved heroes. Katsu starred in twenty-five Zatoichi movies, some shot concurrently with the Hanzo movies, and played him for four seasons on a TV spin-off series. It's as if Lee Majors had starred in a series of R-rated movies about a rape superhero while *The Six Million Dollar Man* was still on the air.

The first Hanzo movie, *Sword of Justice* (1972), sets up the series: Hanzo hears that an infamous murderer has escaped justice, and the evidence suggests complicity at the highest levels . . . In other words, he's got some mistresses to rape. In the second installment, *The Snare* (1973), Hanzo investigates an illegal abortion/currency devaluation ring (yeah, yeah, just go with it) centered around a witchy but still rapeable temple priestess. And in the third movie, *Who's Got the Gold?* (1974), Hanzo foils a plot to embezzle gold from the Shogun himself. And while it isn't quite as good as the first two, *Who's Got the Gold?* does have a scene where Hanzo uses his patented member method on a female ghost after uttering the immortal line, "I want to make love to a ghost once."

SEX AND FURY/FEMALE YAKUZA TALE

Sex and Fury (1973) and *Female Yakuza Tale* (1973) (a.k.a. *Story of a Wild Elder Sister: Widespread Lynch Law*) are both right up there with the Hanzo the Razor movies in the exploitation department. Exploitation movies always have to have a gimmick, and if Hanzo's is his magic penis, then Ocho's is boobs. Specifically, tattooed boobs decorated with cherry blossoms or chrysanthemums or butterflies or whatever. This great pair (pun intended) of movies belongs to the genre of pinky violence, a stimulating hybrid of female-led action and soft-core porn that flourished in Japan in the early 1970s.

Reiko Ike, whose tough-but-sensual vibe would make her an *excellent* blaxploitation movie madam, stars as Inoshika Ocho, a professional gambler with a blood grudge in the late Meiji era (early twentieth century). Ocho's specialty is *hanafuda*, traditional Japanese playing cards decorated with the same plant and animal symbols that adorn our heroine's flesh. *Hanafuda* are used in a number of card games favored by the yakuza, and not only can Ocho play (and cheat at) these games like a boss, when it's time to rumble, her *hanafuda* deck doubles as a weapon, as she throws the cards like a ninja throws a *shuriken*. But the *hanafuda* have another, more personal meaning to Ocho: when she was a young girl, she witnessed the murder of her policeman father, who as he lay dying gave his daughter three bloody *hanafuda* cards—boar, deer, and butterfly—as clues to the identity of his killers.

In *Sex and Fury*, directed by Norifumi Suzuki, Ocho receives a vital lead in tracking down the three men responsible for killing her father. Her twisted path of revenge leads to, among other sexy S&M-tinged adventures, a high-stakes card game with Swedish sexploitation star Christina Lindberg.

The second film, *Female Yakuza Tale*, comes courtesy of Teruo Ishii, a director known for surrealist vignettes that combine the more grotesque aspects of a David Lynch movie with the candy-colored carnage of Lone Wolf and Cub. And in *Female Yakuza Tale*, he delivers the blood and nudity that are the raison d'être for this type of flick, but he does it with such gonzo audacity that it comes off more defiant than lecherous. For example, in the opening scene, Ishii has Ocho battle a large group of swordsmen in the rain. She starts off fully dressed, but as the fight goes on—like a katana-wielding game of strip poker—Ocho's clothes are sliced off a piece at a time. (However, this is nothing compared to *Sex and Fury*'s also completely naked opening scene, where Ocho is interrupted in the bath by *another* large group of fighters.)

The outrageousness continues as Ocho becomes involved with a group of women being victimized by yakuza who force them to smuggle drugs ... in their vaginas (of course). These same women are kept docile by heroin shot directly into their nipples (of course), but when a mysterious trench-coat-clad hit woman and an embittered former gang member come on the scene, Ocho joins forces with them to rally the girls against their tormenters. The movie ends in a showdown that's reminiscent of the House of Blue Leaves massacre . . . except for one little detail. Can you guess what is? I'll give you a hint: the blades aren't the only things that are naked.

BLIND WOMAN'S CURSE

Blind Woman's Curse, a.k.a. *The Tattooed Swordswoman* (1970), teams up *Lady Snowblood*'s Meiko Kaji with *Female Yakuza Tale*'s Teruo Ishii, and the result is a mad, delirious, totally badass hybrid of three uniquely Japanese genres: pinky violence, *kaidan* (traditional ghost stories), and *ninkyo eiga* (chivalrous yakuza) films.

Kaji is young and just developing her stoic persona, but she's perfect as Akemi, the solemn "elder sister" of a spunky gang of teenage swordswomen marked by their matching back tattoos. (When they line up in battle formation, their tattoos come together to form a giant dragon with Akemi as the head.) Years ago, Akemi accidentally blinded the daughter of a rival yakuza in battle. She went to prison for her part in the massacre, but now that she's out, the titular "blind woman" (Hoki Tokuda) is looking for revenge. When the members of Akemi's gang begin to disappear, their dragon tattoos flayed from their backs as grotesque tokens, she (and we) know the time to pay the piper is at hand. And what is with that creepy blood-drinking cat?!

Blind Woman's Curse is a bizarre genre mash-up full of unforgettable baroque imagery, as Ishii brings his "euro-guro" (or "erotic grotesque," an aesthetic we don't really have an equivalent for in the West) flair in the form of an outlandish freak show and nightmarish circus scene that is as gorgeous as it is unsettling. So if you're interested in any of the following: psychedelic visuals, Asian folklore, yakuza, girl gangs, ghost stories, swordplay, and/or tits, then *Blind Woman's Curse* will leave you satisfied.

THE STREETFIGHTER TRILOGY

Terry Tsurugi, Sonny Chiba's character from the Streetfighter movies, *is* the "Man from Okinawa" referred to in *Kill Bill: Volume 1*. Of course, there's also the matter of Chiba himself costarring as master sword maker Hattori Hanzo. Tarantino has been a big fan of Chiba's since he saw him on the TV show *Shadow Warriors*, a.k.a. *Kage no Gundan*, as a kid. *Shadow Warriors* chronicled the adventures of a wandering samurai-for-hire named Hattori Hanzo (definitely not a coincidence) in feudal Japan. As Tarantino explained in a 2003 interview: "Every time they did a new series, it was always a different Hattori Hanzo. It was set a little further in history ... So now Sonny Chiba is playing Hattori Hanzo one hundred and still continuing that character."

But we're getting ahead of ourselves. Sonny Chiba began studying martial arts in his youth and appeared in a number of minor roles in Japanese action flicks throughout the '60s, but it was the rise of "open-hand" fighting flicks (or as we call them, kung fu movies) that gave him the opportunity for his big breakthrough. *The Streetfighter* (1974) represented a new, more intense breed of Asian action hero, one who didn't have the swordplay skills of a Tomisaburo Wakayama or the athletic grace of a Bruce Lee, but instead specialized in eye-gouging, bone-crunching action that made up for in brutality what it lacked in grace.

The Streetfighter is set in an alternate universe that may look like our own but is unencumbered by the laws of physics. So when you're having a conversation and things start to get awkward, just jump out the window onto the back of a passing flatbed truck! Or if a guy comes up to you and challenges you to a fight, just rip his tonsils out! *The Streetfighter* has been condemned for its excessive violence (in fact, it was the first movie rated X for violence), and the action is undeniably *rough*. These aren't intricately choreographed fight-dances, they're honest-to-god beatings, and when we see guys throw up from being hit too hard, it's hard to say if it was in the script or a spontaneous reaction.

In all three films, Terry is a "half-breed" who struggles for acceptance in both the Chinese and Japanese communities. However, he *is* accepted as a professional ass-kicker who specializes in killing men with his bare hands. In *The Streetfighter* (1974), Terry is hired to rescue a murderer named Taketi Shikenbaru (Masashi Ishibashi) from prison and spirit him away to Hong Kong; however, when his siblings fail to produce the rest of Terry's fee, he beats the brother senseless and sells the sister into prostitution. After that, he takes on another assignment rescuing the daughter of a recently deceased oil sheik who has been captured by dope-dealing slimeballs ...but only because those dope-dealing slimeballs are Chinese, and Terry doesn't trust the Chinese.

The sequels, *Return of the Streetfighter* (1974) and *The Streetfighter's Last Revenge* (1974), both chronicle the continuing adventures of Terry and his fists; in the second, he gets a new jive-talking teenybopper sidekick, Kitty (Yoko Ichiji), and busts up a phony charity that's actually a front for the yakuza. In the third, he gets screwed by a gangster over a recipe for super-cheap heroin, so as usual, he's got to whup some ass and get his money.

See also: the Sister Streetfighter movies, which are only tangentially related to *The Streetfighter* and star Etsuko "Sue" Shihomi as a deadly female martial artist.

FEMALE PRISONER SCORPION SERIES

You want to find the most stone-cold female badass in all of movie history? I challenge you to find an assassin any more cold, cool, and calculated than Matsu, a.k.a. Female Prisoner Scorpion. The Scorpion movies all sound irredeemably lurid on paper, but in execution, they transcend their exploitation origins to create something that straddles the line between pure pulp and high art.

This is thanks to the efforts of director Shunya Ito and star Meiko Kaji. Kaji was never quite comfortable with the action-heroine box that she had been placed into, and she resisted the trend in Japanese cinema at the time toward excessive nudity and sexuality (she even left her first employer, Nikkatsu Studios, when they switched to a policy of all soft-core porno, all the time). One of Scorpion's most striking character traits was actually a direct result of Kaji's conservatism: in the comic the movies are based on, Scorpion has the mouth of a sailor, but Kaji was uncomfortable using foul language on screen. So she plays Scorpion practically silent and completely introverted, speaking only when absolutely necessary. But her gigantic eyes are always watching, defiantly throwing the audience's gaze right back at it.

The other half of the equation, Shunya Ito, transcends his status as an exploitation director by virtue of his inventive camera work and striking symbolic imagery. The Scorpion movies are definitely exploitation films, in that you can sense that there's a certain quota of nudity and violence that has to be met, but Ito subverts these expectations by presenting the seedier elements in the most artistic way possible. For example, instead of just turning the camera on a bunch of inmates showering and letting the nudity do the work, as many directors would, Ito takes a sleazy scene of shower shivving and turns it into a Kabuki play. The Scorpion movies are packed with this kind of memorable imagery: the red autumn leaves whirling around Scorpion as she receives her destiny in the form of a sharpened blade in the second movie; hundreds of lit matches gently floating down a dank sewer in the third. If imagery like this were done in any other context, it would be hailed as visual genius of the highest order. (It's really too bad that Ito isn't better known; aside from the Scorpion movies, none of his work ever made it abroad.)

The first Scorpion movie, *Female Prisoner #701: Scorpion* (1972), sets up the back story: Matsu landed in jail thanks to the treachery of her police-officer boyfriend. He not only put her in harm's way by persuading her to go undercover in a narcotics ring, he then stood by (seriously, he's in the next room) and let her get raped in the process. Driven mad by the betrayal, she tries to kill him, but unfortunately, since he's a cop and she tried to get him on his way out of work, she is arrested immediately instead. She ends up in a hellish women's prison, where she gets on the wrong side of both the bitchy queen bees and the warden, ending up tied up and lying on the floor of a damp, windowless cell. But Scorpion endures...
The second film, *Female Prisoner #701 Scorpion: Jailhouse 41* (1972) is even more ambitious and atypical than the first, as Scorpion and a band of female inmates escape from jail and go on a surreal, dreamlike "road trip" across the Japanese countryside, which under Ito's lens looks more like the surface of the moon.

The third and fourth movies, *Female Prisoner #701 Scorpion: Beast Stable* (1973) and *Female Prisoner #701 Scorpion: Grudge Song* (1973) completely change course from the first two, as the jailhouse setting is replaced by the streets of Tokyo. That's not to say Matsu doesn't have run-ins with the law; at the beginning of *Beast Stable*, she cuts off—in one swipe—the forearm of a cop who tries to handcuff himself to her. Law successfully averted, Matsu tries to go straight and gets a job at a sewing factory. But there are just too many abusive lowlifes around (including one of her rivals from the first movie, now out of jail and working as a madam), and so, once

again, it's time for some revenge. Finally, *Grudge Song* opens with
the cops interrupting a Western-style wedding and ambushing one
of the guests ... guess who? They catch Matsu but can't keep her
for long, and while on the run, she meets a kindred spirit in Kudo,
a projectionist at a porno theater who also has a grudge against
authority. *Grudge Song* was directed by Yasuharu Hasebe, not Shunya
Ito, and so isn't as good as the first three movies. However, it's full of
daring escapes and has some pretty cool scenes, especially the last
one ... but you're just going to have to check that out for yourself.

Over the course of this four-film cycle (there are more, but don't
bother), Matsu evolves from a regular woman victimized by her lover
into a superhuman assassin. The battle of the sexes is quite literal in
the Scorpion movies, and they can get very, very dark at times, with
all men portrayed as varying shades of awful as they drive women
to madness and murder. But the movies come down firmly on the
women's side, supporting their right to revolution. They also ridicule
and humiliate (invariably male) authority figures every chance they
get, broadening the conflict from men versus women to oppressors
versus oppressed. And Scorpion looms over them all as the avenging
goddess, the one who defends those who can't defend themselves.
So whether you're a sadistic warden or a rapist pimp, if you hurt
women, watch out—Scorpion may have been hurt once, but she
can't be hurt anymore, and she is coming for you.

WAR OF THE GARGANTUAS

There could be (and have been) volumes written on *kaiju eiga*, the
beloved genre of Japanese "giant monster rampages through a
major metropolitan area" movies that begins with *Godzilla* (1954)
but certainly doesn't end there. The *kaiju* experience is usually on
a level with something from *Mystery Science Theater 3000*—rubber
suits, fighter jets dangling from strings, hilariously bad dubbing and
all. But *War of the Gargantuas* (1968) is an altogether more thought-
provoking experience, thanks to a remastered DVD from Classic
Media that includes the original Japanese audio track with English
subtitles. And when you watch it in Japanese, new levels of meaning
emerge ...

Just kidding. It's two guys in giant Bigfoot-meets-the-Creature-from-20,000-Leagues suits, "brothers" who were *spawned from the discarded cells of a giant Frankenstein's monster* at the end of the first film (oh, by the way...this is a sequel. Its predecessor is 1965's *Frankenstein Conquers the World*). And not only do the twosome look nothing like Frankenstein as we (or the Japanese for that matter) know him, they are also complete opposites of one another. One, Gaira the green Sea Gargantua (or "Frankenstein"), is a bloodthirsty monster who fights an enormous kraken, terrorizes Haneda airport, and snatches up a pretty foreign singer right in the middle of an abysmal musical number. (Actually, all that is pretty cool, but you get the point.) The other, Sanda the brown Mountain Gargantua, was raised in captivity by our scientist-heroes (including a young Russ Tamblyn, who appears in the film for reasons unknown seemingly even to himself) and is a mellow pacifist type. But alas, Sanda's attempts to talk it out with his thirty-foot brother are unsuccessful, and the two duke it out in a gargantuan (eh? ehhhh?) battle that destroys a sizable chunk of Tokyo.

Metaphor for nuclear war? Probably. Grown men in silly costumes stomping on tiny towns made of plywood? Definitely. But give it a chance—after all, Brad Pitt said at the 2012 Academy Awards that this was the movie that got him into acting, and Tarantino famously ordered his staff to build a miniature version of Tokyo as an homage to it while shooting *Kill Bill: Volume 1*. He's also stated that he screened *War of the Gargantuas* for Daryl Hannah on set (bonus points if you can spot the reference in her "black mamba" speech) and envisioned the battle between Elle Driver and The Bride as a "War of the Blonde Gargantuas." So c'mon. You know you love it.

KINJI FUKASAKU

Kill Bill is dedicated to Japanese film director Kinji Fukasaku, whose gritty, realistic *Battles Without Honor and Humanity* movies are regarded in Japan like *The Godfather* is in the US. The first movie, *Battles Without Honor and Humanity*, came out in 1973 and spawned four sequels (seven if you count *New Battles Without Honor and*

Humanity) to form a sprawling, intricately detailed epic chronicling the rise of a new breed of yakuza—one without *jingi*, translated as "honor and humanity"—in post–World War II Osaka.

But there's definitely more to Fukasaku than the *Battles* movies: He directed sixty-six films in his forty-year career, including the Japanese sequences of *Tora! Tora! Tora!* (1970); Sonny Chiba movies such as *Doberman Dekka* (1977), another Japanese-style *Dirty Harry*; the insane mythological samurai film *Samurai Reincarnation* (1981), featuring set design that would make Tim Burton jealous; and *Black Lizard* (1968), starring Japanese drag queen Akihiro Miwa as a psychedelic transvestite jewel thief prone to high-camp pronouncements such as, "People would be more beautiful if they were more like diamonds...without souls."

However, he is best known in the US for one of his final films, *Battle Royale* (2000). *Battle Royale* was a smash hit when it was released in Japan in 2000, but it wasn't officially available in America until 2012, when distributors finally allowed it to be released on DVD and Blu-ray. (The irony is that *Battle Royale* was already a well-known movie among cult film fans by the time of its "official" release, thanks to healthy word of mouth and brisk trade on the bootleg and import circuits.) Why did they wait so long to release *Battle Royale* stateside? Reportedly, they anticipated backlash from viewers, whom they feared would find it in bad taste in the "Columbine era." And why 2012? Well, they may have finally been reassured by the popularity of a little book called *The Hunger Games*, which (ahem) *liberally borrows* from *Battle Royale*.

The premise is that in the near future, juvenile delinquency has gotten so far out of hand that the government has instituted an annual event called the "Battle Royale" to keep rebellious teenagers in line. Every year, a graduating class is chosen by lottery and herded onto a bus, supposedly to go on their senior trip; however, en route the kids are gassed and spirited away to an isolated island where the "game" will be played. All students are fitted with exploding collars around their necks, given a duffel bag full of random weapons (some get machine guns, some get pot lids), and told that they have forty-eight hours to kill their classmates or be killed themselves. And if they refuse? *Boom!* goes the collar.

Battle Royale is equal parts dystopian commentary on the generation gap and the movie equivalent of a video game as the students take each other down one by one, complete with a running tally of the body count. All manner of high school stereotypes make their appearances, such as Chiaki Kuriyama (a.k.a. GoGo Yubari) as tracksuit-clad jock Takako, Ko Shibasaki as vengeful class slut Mitsuko, and our protagonists Tatsuya Fujiwara and Aki Maeda as the sensitive Shuya and his secret crush Noriko. And Renaissance man Beat Takeshi, who is known both as an amiable TV comedian and the director of ultraviolent yakuza movies (such as *Outrage* [2011], also highly recommended) is spot-on as the droll but sadistic "Teacher" running the game.

Unfortunately, *Battle Royale* was Fukasaku's last proper film; he died while directing the sequel, and the result is a haphazard, uneven affair. But *Battle Royale* itself works spectacularly both as a black comedy and an action movie, boasting highly professional direction and slick editing and production values. It almost goes without saying that it's extremely violent, but it's got a witty sensibility that is positively Tarantino-esque. And according to Tarantino, that was no accident. As he told the Japanese film magazine *Eiga Hi-Ho* in a 2003 interview: "I went out to dinner with Kinji Fukasaku and Kenta (Kinji's son), and I was going, 'Man, I love this movie! It is just so fantastic!' And I said, 'I love the scene where the girls are shooting each other.' And then Kenta starts laughing. So I ask, 'Why are you laughing?' He goes, 'The author of the original *Battle Royale* novel would be very happy to hear that you liked that scene.' And I go, 'Why?' And he says, 'Well, because it's from *Reservoir Dogs*!'"

TAKASHI MIIKE

Japanese director Takashi Miike has always been there, hovering in the background, throughout Tarantino's career. And when he was on the press tour to promote his protégé Eli Roth's movie *Hostel* in 2005, Tarantino told *New York* magazine, "Man, it all started with Takashi Miike."

Unlike Tarantino, Miike is highly prolific. It's unfair to compare the two, though, because very few directors, period, are as prolific as Miike—as of early 2012, he has directed an astounding eighty-eight movies in twenty-one years, with another one on the way. Miike has always operated under a system where he churns out three or four direct-to-video stinkers in order to raise money for his passion projects, which to put it bluntly are some of the weirdest shit you've ever seen in your life. This approach to filmmaking means that you've got to do your homework before you dive in to Miike; he's made a little of everything (contrast his sweet-natured 2011 kids' flick *Ninja Kids!!!* with his deranged 2001 movie *Visitor Q*, in which a man solves the dilemma of having his penis stuck inside a dead body in the grips of rigor mortis by shooting himself full of heroin), and not all of it is good. He's known primarily for his ultraviolent yakuza and horror movies, such as *Ichi the Killer* (2001), about a masochistic yakuza and the budding psycho killer who's bumping off his colleagues; and *Audition* (1999), a masterful example of slow-burn horror about a lonely widower who holds "auditions" for a new girlfriend, only to discover that the "perfect woman" he meets in the process is not what she seems. (Both are highly recommended for Tarantino fans by the way; also check out his gory gangster flick *Dead or Alive*, 1999, and his bizarre 2001 zombie musical, *Happiness of the Katakuris*.)

Tarantino and Miike finally got the chance to work together in 2007, when Tarantino played a gunfighter named Ringo in *Sukiyaki Western Django*, Miike's *Kill Bill*–style tribute to the spaghetti Western genre. *Sukiyaki Western Django* is basically a remake of *Django* (see chapter 8), which is ironic, considering *Django* was a remake of the 1961 Japanese samurai movie *Yojimbo*. So it's a Japanese remake of an Italian remake of a Japanese movie, and as if that weren't crazy enough, Miike had his Japanese cast deliver their lines in phonetic English, so they have no idea what they're saying.

Miike has gained a veneer of art-house credibility in recent years with his dark, bloody samurai dramas *13 Assassins* (2010) and *Hara-Kiri: Death of a Samurai* (2011), but as long as he's got ideas like *Sukiyaki Western Django* up his sleeve, you better believe that this wild man of Japanese cinema will, at the very least, never become boring.

ACT OF VENGEANCE: THE RAPE/REVENGE CYCLE

There are lots of movies about revenge. Most of the movies in this book are about revenge in one way or another. But there's one subgenre that approaches the subject in an especially nasty way. The rape/revenge cycle is a series of exploitation movies, usually American but not necessarily, that still exists today but was especially common in the '70s. Rape/revenge is used as a trope in a variety of stories (*The Girl with the Dragon Tattoo*, anybody?), but all true rape/revenge movies follow the same three-act structure: woman gets raped; woman transforms herself into a badass; woman kills her victimizer(s), usually brutally and with extreme prejudice. It's the last two parts that lend this particular subgenre to a feminist interpretation, though it really depends on whether the movie is more focused on the rape or the revenge.

It originated with art-house director Ingmar Bergman, whose *The Virgin Spring* (1960) was remade as *Last House on the Left* (1972) by future "Master of Horror" Wes Craven. These two movies follow the same plot, but with one key twist: in *The Virgin Spring*, one innocent young girl is brutally raped and left for dead, and in *Last House on the Left*, there are two. They both hinge on the same serendipitous twist, though: the rapists end up seeking shelter with the parents of the girl they violated.

Virgin Spring and *Last House* are atypical, since it's the girls' parents, not the girls themselves, who rain vengeance down on her attackers. Another atypical example is *Rape Squad* (1974), which goes all *Charlie's Angels* with the concept by teaming up five model-gorgeous women who have all suffered at the hands of the "Jingle Bell Rapist," so called because he makes his victims sing "Jingle

Bells" while he rapes them. (Really.) *Rape Squad* is odd because it combines a militant feminist script with a titty-flick aesthetic, leading to scenes such as our heroines planning their vigilante activities while soaking topless in a hot tub.

I Spit on Your Grave (1978), on the other hand, is the concept distilled down to its most archetypal form: the striking Camille Keaton (granddaughter of silent-film comedian Buster Keaton) stars as Jennifer, a writer looking for some peace and quiet to finish her new book. She rents an isolated cabin out in the woods, but when she arrives, she's greeted by a brutal gang of redneck thugs. They gang-rape her and beat her bloody, but Jennifer refuses to die. Instead she picks herself up, cleans herself off, and systematically hunts down and kills every last one of those fuckers. (She even castrates one of them!) *I Spit on Your Grave* is cheap looking and highly explicit in both sex and violence, and boasts one of the most sensationalized taglines ever: "This woman has just cut, chopped, broken, and burned five men beyond recognition...but no jury in America would ever convict her!" Keaton also does a great job evoking sympathy for her character's anguished mental state, but it walks a very fine line.

That line was crossed for Swedish sexploitation actress Christina Lindberg (*Sex and Fury*) when the director of *Thriller: A Cruel Picture*, a.k.a. *They Call Her One Eye* (1974) inserted hardcore penetration shots performed by a body double into the movie without telling her. She was deeply disillusioned by the experience and ended up quitting acting to become a journalist not long afterward. And it's a shame, too, because Christina's performance in *Thriller* as a mute in a leather duster with one "big, beautiful eye," who totes a shotgun nearly as big as she is, is positively iconic. The Elle Driver reference is obvious; as Tarantino told *Eiga Hi-Ho* magazine back in 2003, "I love Christina Lindberg. And that's definitely who Daryl Hannah's character is based on ... Just like They Call Her One Eye, she's got some color coordinated eye patches. And that is, of all the revenge movies I've ever seen,...definitely the roughest. There's never been anything as tough as that movie."

"Tough" is an understatement. *Thriller: A Cruel Picture* is as nihilistic and bleak as they come. Things go from bad to worse for Lindberg's character over the course of the film, and even bloody revenge is poor compensation for how completely these bastards have shattered her world. She's been kidnapped, hooked on smack, and forced to work as a prostitute. The one bright spot in her miserable existence is that she (apparently?) doesn't have to turn tricks on the weekends, time she devotes to shooting and stunt-driving lessons. When one of her eyes is ripped out as discipline from her captors, it only strengthens her resolve to send these fuckers straight to hell...and she does. Oh, how she does.

As the '70s turned into the '80s, the rape/revenge cycle changed location from the wilderness to the urban jungle. Abel Ferrara (See chapter 1) threw his hat into the ring with *Ms. 45* (1981), starring Zoe Lund as another mute who declares war on the male of the species after being brutally raped—twice—on the streets of New York; the movie culminates with our heroine crashing a Halloween party in a nun's habit, her trusty .45 in hand. *Savage Streets* (1984) stars former "*Exorcist* kid" Linda Blair as a big-haired, catsuit-clad teen vigilante who hunts down the punks (no really, they're punk rockers) who killed her best friend and raped her mute (*again!*) sister. The '80s production design makes *Savage Streets* occasionally resemble a sleaze-cinema version of the "Love is a Battlefield" video, spiced up with plenty of nudity, cheesy one-liners, foul language, and death by crossbow.

In the '90s, *A Gun for Jennifer* (1997) attempted to inject some riot grrrl defiance into the rape/revenge formula, smashing any lingering ambiguity about the filmmaker's intentions with the tagline "Dead men don't rape." And in the twenty-first century, there have been a smattering of movies utilizing the rape/revenge structure, including the widely banned French movie *Baise-moi* (2000), translated alternately as *Kiss Me*, *Fuck Me,* and *Rape Me*; and *Irreversible* (2002), the debut of *Enter the Void* (2009)'s Gaspar Noe. *Irreversible* made waves (to say the least) on the art-house circuit by portraying the graphic anal rape of famous Italian sexpot Monica Bellucci. The neo-exploitation trend of the late 2000s has also seen its share of rape/revenge revivals, most of them completely abysmal. One effort, the charmingly titled *Run! Bitch Run!* (2009), harkens back to rape/revenge's "golden age" of the late '70s, when according to the official synopsis, "the lack of modern technology made the world a more vulnerable place." And it's true—communications technology has irrevocably altered one of rape/revenge's most hallowed tropes. It's easier to leave someone for dead when she can't call for help on her cell phone.

(Author's Collection.)

5

KILL BILL: VOLUME 2:
THE WHOLE BLOODY AFFAIR

Whenever people talk about the *Kill Bill* movies, they tend to focus on the *Lady Snowblood*s and the *Sex and Fury*s and forget about all of the other elements that went into the film. And if you want to talk formative influences, the kind of movie-going experiences that made Tarantino the obsessive fan he is today, then there are two elements of *Kill Bill* that are even more important than Japanese exploitation: kung fu movies and Italian horror. (*Kill Bill: Volume 2* in particular also draws heavily from spaghetti Westerns, but we'll get into those later.)

See, most of the Japanese exploitation we talked about just now didn't make it to America until decades later, but kung fu and Italian horror were staples on the B-movie circuit back in the '70s. And once again, as with blaxploitation, who had his skinny teenaged ass parked in those (one can only presume) horribly uncomfortable seats? A young Tarantino. As he told *Entertainment Weekly* in 2006: "As soon as I got old enough to look like I could get into an R-rated movie, I'd go to the ghetto theater in my neighborhood—the Carson Twin Cinema in Carson, Calif.— and I saw every kung fu movie that came out from '76 on, every Italian horror film ... I would sit through movies I didn't even care for three times."

Kung fu was introduced to America during the heyday of the grindhouse circuit, and Hong Kong imports screened regularly at inner-city theaters throughout the '70s. They were particularly popular in New York, where theaters on the notorious 42nd Street strip would play them around the clock to crowds of enthusiastic minority youths; these same kids, when they weren't cheering on kung fu stars such as Gordon Liu, were busy inventing break dancing (which worked kung fu inspired moves into its routines) and hip hop (where else did you think the Wu-Tang Clan got its name?)

The kung fu phenomenon was by no means restricted to these subcultures, however. With Hong Kong imports such as Lo Lieh and Bruce Lee providing the spark, the TV show *Kung Fu*, starring David Carradine as the half-Chinese, half-American Shaolin monk Kwai Chang Caine, exploded into a full-on cultural force when it debuted in 1972. Thus by casting Carradine alongside Sonny Chiba and Gordon Liu in *Kill Bill* did Tarantino complete the Holy Trinity of martial arts from its Japanese and Chinese forefathers to their American acolytes.

Giallo didn't make as big of an impression as kung fu in the American collective unconscious and remains a cult phenomenon outside of its native Italy, but you can clearly see its influence in *Kill Bill*. You can especially see it in the sickly fluorescent lighting of the hospital sequence in *Volume 1*, in the reflexive twitch of rapist orderly Buck's leg as he dies. *Giallo* is shorthand for any kind of thriller in Italy, but the term as we're using it (it's a tricky one to pronounce—like "jello" with a long "ah") refers to a certain highly stylized type of movie that was very influential in the creation of the "slasher" genre.

Giallo means "yellow" in Italian, and the term comes from the yellow covers of a series of murder mystery novels introduced to Italy in the late 1920s. As a film genre, *giallo* is hard to pin down, but generally it amps up the style of Alfred Hitchcock (who, without exception, all *giallo* directors adore) for a whodunit mystery featuring stylish, utlraviolent murder sequences and liberal amounts of sex and nudity. *Giallo* usually has a female protagonist (often a foreigner), and fetishizes female beauty even as it continually undermines female credibility (the heroines are often believed to be "crazy," and hallucination sequences are also common). These sensual fever dreams of knives, beautiful women, and knives in beautiful women also often include psychedelic color schemes and highly stylized production design, but at the same time, many of the most famous *giallo* don't follow these rules. *Giallo* is more of a vague sensibility than a cinematic formula—one of those "you'll know it when you see it" things—and to make it even more complicated, some of the masters of *giallo*'s best and most famous works aren't *giallos* at all. So to keep things simple, we're just going to talk about the "big three" of Italian horror directors—Mario Bava, Dario Argento, and Lucio Fulci—in whose filmographies you'll find the basics of *giallo*. Okay? Okay! Now enough of this crap, let's get to the violence!

CHINESE BOXER, A.K.A. THE HAMMER OF GOD

Chinese Boxer, a.k.a. *The Hammer of God* (1970) is the OG (that's "original gangster," squares) of kung fu movies. A landmark film and a favorite of Tarantino's, this is the flick that introduced the world to the "open hand" style of fighting. Oh sure, there had been *wuxia* (martial arts) movies made in Hong Kong since the movies first came to Hong Kong, but *Chinese Boxer* broke all of the rules. It was the first *wuxia* movie where the hero didn't fight with a sword but with his hands, and thus, with a nauseating punch in the gut, what we know today as the "kung fu movie" was born.

Jimmy Wang Yu was ever so briefly the king of kung fu before his fame was eclipsed by "The Dragon" Bruce Lee, and like Lee, Yu peddled his own revolutionary blend of kung fu, karate, samurai, and traditional *wuxia* styles. Also, like Bruce Lee's 1972 movie *The Chinese Connection*, *Chinese Boxer* is a shamelessly jingoistic bit of flag waving that seeks to exploit the ancient rivalry between the Chinese and Japanese for maximum bone-crunching, eye-gouging effect. Many elements of *Chinese Boxer* may seem horribly cliché when you first see it, particularly its climactic "1 vs. 100" final battle sequence, but you've got to understand one thing: this is where those clichés *came from*. To wit:

A cocky dickhead comes to challenge an entire kung fu school to a fight, only to be put in his place by the master in charge. But being a cocky dickhead, the challenger refuses to accept defeat and brings in Japanese karate expert/hired thug Kita (Lo Lieh) to terrorize the school some more. The resultant bloodbath leaves only one survivor, a student named Lei Ming (Jimmy Wang Yu). Does Lei Ming then go underground and transform himself into an untouchable badass to get revenge for his slain comrades? You bet he does! *Chinese Boxer* is that simple, and that profound. The icing on this cake (a cake shaped like a fist, of course) is that now that he's a superhuman assassin type, Lei Ming dons a surgeon's mask and rubber gloves before every fight. Why? Because he's a doctor now. A doctor of *death*.

FIVE FINGERS OF DEATH, A.K.A. KING BOXER

Alongside Bruce Lee and Kung Fu's David Carradine, *Five Fingers of Death*, a.k.a. *King Boxer* (1972), from director Cheng Chang Ho is responsible for bringing the kung fu phenomenon to American shores. *Five Fingers of Death* is a take-no-prisoners action flick full of exuberantly supernatural touches guaranteed to bring an audience to its feet.

Chief among these is the tendency for star Lo Lieh's palm to glow red every time he uses his top-secret "Five Fingers of Death" Iron Fist heart-stopping technique, accompanied by that famous sound effect (it's hard to describe—kind of like a police siren— you'll definitely know it when you hear it) that was sampled in *Kill Bill: Volume 1*. Interestingly, the sound effect didn't originate with this movie either: it's actually sampled from the theme to *Ironside*, a late-'60s/early-'70s TV series about a wheelchair-bound detective. When *Five Fingers of Death* first played in urban theaters, people would laugh—*Ironside* was still on the air at the time—but would invariably rally around that distinctive screech by the end of the movie. As Tarantino says in a 2003 interview with the Japanese film magazine *Eiga Hi-Ho*: "So every time the screen would glow, people in the audience would bust up laughing because it was the *Ironside* theme. But at a certain point, they actually begin to like it better in the movie. By the third time they hear it, the audience is going 'YEAH! KICK ASS LO LIEH!' I think it works great. And in *Bill*, the third time you hear it, you know she's going to kick ass!"

The plot concerns Chao Chi Hao (Lo Lieh, playing the good guy this time), an outstanding and loyal kung fu student who lives with his adopted father and his niece. After thugs in the employ of a local warlord victimize his elderly father, Chao is sent away for advanced training with a friend of the family Shen Chin Pei (Mien Fang) so he can learn to protect himself and his kin. But before his bags are even packed, Chao Chi Hao gets caught up in a fight with the warlord's henchmen, who are trying to kidnap Shen Chin Pei's daughter. Although his style is still unrefined, Chao does manage to rescue the lady, and *now* he and his new master's daughter can head off to the martial arts school.

When Chao first arrives, kung fu master Shen Chin Pei ridicules Chao's technique, telling him that he will work as a janitor and be happy about it because he is not yet worthy to receive instruction in the mystic arts of kung fu. But Chao is determined, and like Beatrix in *Kill Bill: Volume 2*, he stoically takes everything Shen can dish out and quickly becomes the master's most promising student. Impressed with his abilities, Chen Chin Pei takes Chao aside and secretly teaches him the deadly "Five Fingers of Death" Iron Fist heart-stopping technique, which he demonstrates to impressive effect when he finally gets to show that asshole warlord and his minions who's boss.

MASTER OF THE FLYING GUILLOTINE

First of all, you can't even begin to talk about *Master of the Flying Guillotine* (1976) without talking about its famous theme music, a funky-yet-terrifying track that comes from the most unlikely of places: the experimental Krautrock band Neu!. It's pretty miraculous that director Jimmy Wang Yu had heard of Neu! at all, since they were positively obscure even in their homeland of Germany at the time. But he did, and he used the menacing song "Super 16" (Google it) as his titular Master's theme (without the band's knowledge, by the way), a move that Tarantino then paid homage to in turn by including "Super 16" on the *Kill Bill* soundtrack:

The lucky schmuck who gets to have "Super 16" play every

time he steps onscreen is Fung Sheng Wu Chi, a.k.a. Master of the Flying Guillotine (Kang Chin), an elderly monk whose students were killed in a confrontation with the One-Armed Boxer (Jimmy Wang Yu). Fung Sheng Wu Chi has been out of the kung fu game for a while, but when he hears of his students' untimely demise, he pulls his trusty Flying Guillotine (a device resembling a red hat, or maybe a lemon juicer, lined with nasty-looking piranha teeth at the end of a long chain) out of storage. And even though he went blind in the interim, it turns out that Fung Sheng Wu Chi hasn't lost his touch, and so he sets out to find this one-armed mystery man and get some bloody vengeance for his students.

Meanwhile the One-Armed Boxer is being pestered by his students to show off his supernatural strength and agility in a kung fu tournament that's being hosted by a neighboring school. He isn't interested, but eventually he agrees to attend the tournament as an observer. A good chunk of *Master of the Flying Guillotine* consists of the tournament itself as we observe matches between an eclectic and sometimes comical mix of fighters, including a Japanese samurai dressed in a kimono and straw hat, and an Indian yogi who can extend his arms to twice his height, Stretch Armstrong style.

Then, suddenly ...*Oh shit! It's Fung Sheng Wu Chi!* The audience scatters when this famous and feared master appears atop a battlement, but Fung Sheng Wu Chi's aim is true as he decapitates a one-armed fighter with a swift tug of his chain. One problem, though: it might have been *a* one-armed boxer, but it wasn't *the* One-Armed Boxer, and Fung Sheng Wu Chi has killed the wrong guy. (This is actually only one of several times this happens. Whoopsy!) But the One-Armed Boxer has seen Fung Sheng Wu Chi's dramatic entrance and knows that it's his head the blind monk wants to collect.

Master of the Flying Guillotine is jam packed with inventive setups and clever twists, which combined with its high-quality fight scenes and endearingly nutty concept make it quite possibly the most entertaining kung fu movie of them all.

THE 36TH CHAMBER OF SHAOLIN

Yep, these are the 36 Chambers that the Wu-Tang Clan were referring to on the album *Enter the Wu-Tang (36 Chambers)*. *The 36th Chamber of Shaolin* (1978), directed by Lau Kar-Leung aka Chia-Liang Liu, has come to define the kung-fu style of the Shaw Brothers in popular culture, and while it wasn't the first kung fu movie to use the "training for vengeance" trope by any stretch of the imagination (its plot is quite similar to that of *Five Fingers of Death*, actually), many people say it's the best. It's certainly one of the most famous...

The 36th Chamber of Shaolin stars a young Gordon Liu at the beginning of his transition from supporting player to leading man. He plays San Te, a martial arts student who sets out to become a kung fu master so he can (what else?) get revenge. San Te is a mere youth when his father is killed by one of the cruel "Generals" whose abuse of power is a plague upon the land. He and his brother decide to go to the famous Shaolin Temple to learn kung fu and avenge their father, but before the siblings can get to their destination, the General's men find them. They kill his brother and badly injure San Te; he makes it to the temple, but when he gets there, the Masters of Shaolin tell him that before he can become a student there, he's going to have to do some bitch work. He must perform manual labor around the temple for a full year before he can even step into the first of the 35 Chambers of Shaolin, each containing a new training challenge. San Te turns out to be a natural and finishes the 35 Chambers in record time, but before he can create his own *36th* chamber of Shaolin, he's got some warlord ass to kick.

FIST OF THE WHITE LOTUS

Okay, so, stay with me here: in *Kill Bill: Volume 2*, Gordon Liu plays the white-haired kung fu master Pai Mei. But in 1977, he fought Pai Mei in *Executioners from Shaolin* before taking on his twin brother Priest White Brows in 1980's *Fist of the White Lotus*, a.k.a. *Clan of the White Lotus*. *Fist of the White Lotus* was directed by Lo Lieh, whom you'll remember from *Chinese Boxer* and *Five Fingers of Death*, and while it is a sequel to *Executioners from Shaolin*, it's also a superior film in nearly every way. The villain is more villainous, the hero more heroic, and the action more action-packed; the only bad parts of *Fist of the White Lotus* are the insufferable attempts at comedy (an unfortunate side effect of Jackie Chan's success that reverberated across the entire Hong Kong film industry), but other than that, it's all good.

Pai Mei gets killed at the end of *Executioners from Shaolin* (a scene that we see repeated here), but you'd be forgiven for thinking that the villain in this movie, Priest White Brows, was the same guy. He looks like Pai Mei, acts like Pai Mei, talks like Pai Mei, and fights like Pai Mei, which I guess is what happens when you set out to make a sequel and realize that you killed off the best part of the movie at the end of the last one. And so Pai...er, Priest White Brows is also the best part of *Fist of the White Lotus*, as Lo Lieh (doing double duty as actor and director) hams it up by challenging all comers from atop his gilded temple fortress. (This gilded temple fortress comes complete with a luxurious Caligula-style bathtub with flower petals sprinkled on the surface of the perfumed water; does this mean we're going to get to see a naked bathtub fight? Yes. Yes it does.)

In the first scene of *Fist of the White Lotus*, Hung Wen-Ting (Gordon Liu) and his comrade Brother Biu (Lin Hui-hang) kill the nefarious Pai Mei by combining tiger- and crane-style kung fu. Enraged by the death of his brother, Priest White Brows then shows up at their temple school and proceeds to kill everything within killing range with his unique style of fighting, which combines a seemingly supernatural ability to dodge his opponents' attacks with a strike hard enough to make their eyeballs bleed. Oh, and he can suck his genitals up into his body. No big. Brother Biu is killed in the conflict, but Hung manages to escape with his brother's widow, Mei-Hsiao (Kara Hui), and the two go into hiding so Hung can perfect his tiger/crane hybrid style of kung fu and defeat the evil Priest White Brows once and for all!

There's just one problem—no matter how hard he trains, Hung's aggressive style can't defeat Priest White Brows, who can manipulate the air around him and just weightlessly floats away from the hardest of blows. (All that dick grabbing isn't going to help either, for reasons I've mentioned above.) Lucky for Hung, he's got a secret weapon under his very roof. Mei-Hsiao is a master of the delicate and graceful art of "women's kung fu," and as she patiently explains to her hard-headed comrade, only a light touch can defeat a light touch. (The training montage where Hung learns daintiness by doing "women's work" such as babysitting, cooking, and embroidery is an absolute riot.) But that's not all, y'all—*Fist of the White Lotus* does an excellent job of keeping the energy up throughout with artistically shot sequences of some of the strangest kung fu you're ever going to see, including acupuncture technique, one-hundred-step soul-catching technique, and five-point-palm-exploding heart technique (yes, the same one that finally killed Bill!)

BRUCE LEE

The 36th Chamber of Shaolin might be the most famous Shaw Brothers movie, but Bruce Lee was the most famous martial artist of all time, period. His career was unfortunately short; Bruce Lee died very young under mysterious circumstances. (The official story is that he was killed by an allergic reaction to the painkiller Equagesic. But conspiracy theories, from an execution ordered by the Chinese mafia to a delayed reaction to a deadly Dim Mak pressure point strike, abound.) However, the movies he did do were enough to make him an icon at home in Hong Kong and abroad. Lee studied many martial arts styles but favored a mixed form of his own invention called Jeet Kune Do, which was based on his philosophy that traditional kung fu was too rigid to be of any use in street fighting.

Born in America but raised in Hong Kong, Lee was the son of a famous stage actor and an aristocrat, but he still knew a thing or three about delivering a beating. Post–World War II Hong Kong was a rough place full of violence and gang warfare, and after young Lee got into some fights, his parents enrolled him in martial arts classes so he could defend himself. Still, Lee's pugilistic nature shone through, and after he beat up the son of a notorious Triad leader, his parents sent him to San Francisco for his own safety. He then spent a few years moving up and down the West Coast teaching his own brand of martial arts before landing the role of Kato on the original *Green Hornet.*

The success of *The Green Hornet* opened some pocketbooks back in Hong Kong, so Lee then returned home for his first starring role in *The Big Boss,* aka *Fists of Fury* (1971). Lee plays a Chinese immigrant in Hong Kong who, along with his cousins, gets caught up in the drug trade. The movie was an enormous box-office success across Asia and catapulted Bruce Lee to stardom; seeing dollar signs, producers rushed to give him funding for *Fist of Fury,* a.k.a. *The Chinese Connection* (1972), which broke the box-office records that had been set by *The Big Boss.* The movie plays on the age-old China/Japan rivalry by casting Lee as Chen Zhen, a martial arts student who defends the honor of his school, his master, and his people against a dastardly gang of villainous Japanese.

With two box-office smashes under his belt, Lee was given complete control as the writer, director, star, and choreographer of the fight scenes for his third film, *Way of the Dragon* (1972). Lee plays Tang Lung, a Chinese martial arts expert sent to Rome to help some friends of his family whose restaurant is being squeezed by the Mafia. (Is there any ethnicity Brice Lee hasn't symbolically kicked in the collective ass?) In *Way of the Dragon*, Lee introduced Chuck Norris (and I know you've heard of Chuck Norris) to the world as his opponent in the final fight at the Roman Coliseum, one of the most memorable fight scenes in martial arts movie history.

In late 1972, Lee began work on his fourth Golden Harvest Film, *Game of Death.* He began filming some scenes, including a fight with 7′2″ American basketball star and former student Kareem Abdul-Jabbar, but production was halted when Warner Brothers came along and offered Lee way more money to star in *Enter the Dragon* (1973). Lee stars as, uh, Lee, a martial arts expert charged with an undercover mission: enter a tournament being held by a martial arts school/Bond-style supervillain compound led by the slippery Han (Shih Kien), exposing their dirty dealings in the drug trade and whipping a ton of ass in the process.

Enter the Dragon enjoyed a rapturous reception from audiences worldwide, but sadly the movie's star never got to enjoy any of its notoriety. Only a few months after its completion and only six days before its July 26, 1973, release date, Bruce Lee died suddenly. Before he died, Lee had shot over one hundred hours of footage for *Game of Death*, including a climactic final battle in the yellow-and-black track suit now more commonly referred to as a "*Kill Bill* costume." So in a controversial move, *Enter the Dragon* director Robert Clouse finished *Game of Death* using a Bruce Lee look-alike, and finally released the film in 1978.

After Lee's untimely death arose the phenomenon of Brucesploitation, where imitators such as Bruce Li, Bruce Le, Dragon Lee, and Bruce Leung (the list goes on and on) just kind of failed to mention on the posters for their movies that no, they weren't the "real" Bruce Lee. Caveat Emptor, I guess. Some highlights of this questionably ethical genre are *The Clones of Bruce Lee* (1981), where all the Bruce impersonators come together to cash one check ... uh, for one cause; and *The Dragon Lives Again* (1976), where the soul of Bruce Lee teams up with Popeye to take on an evil gang that includes Dracula, James Bond, Clint Eastwood, the Godfather, and Euro-porn star Emmanuelle!

MARIO BAVA

Like a suburban teen fated to take over his father's Mazda dealership, Mario Bava was born to become the "old master" of *giallo*. His father was a pioneering special-effects artist in the early days of Italian cinema, and after attending art school, young Mario began working as a cinematographer. Even after he moved into directing, Bava treated his movies as pieces of art first and stories second. Bava movies convey their messages largely through light, color, and setting, with the plot seemingly little more than a device to string together a series of beautiful, bloody set pieces. Also thanks to his origins in cinematography, Bava's films are known for their intricate and ambitious camera work, made even more impressive considering Italian movies often didn't have sync sound at the time, let alone expensive equipment such as dolly tracks and cranes.

He made his directorial debut with the black-and-white

gothic horror flick *Black Sunday* (1960), a tale of witchcraft set in seventeenth-century Moldova that made future *Hammer House of Horror* queen Barbara Steele a star. Then after a few diversions into the mythology-based peplum genre (including the surreal *Hercules in the Haunted World*, which aficionados consider among the genre's best), Bava returned to atmospheric horror with the anthology film *Black Sabbath* (1962). (Which, by the way, is *totally* where Ozzy and Tony Iommi got the name.) Like *Pulp Fiction*, *Black Sabbath* is a triptych, but unlike *Pulp*, the stories don't intersect. Bava scooped *When a Stranger Calls* (1979) by over a decade with the movie's first segment, "The Telephone," where an attractive young woman is terrorized by sinister phone calls in modern-day Rome; in the second, "I Wurdulak," he put a unique folkloric spin on the vampire story with horror icon Boris Karloff; and in the third, "A Drop of Water," he stayed true to the gothic ghost story with the tale of a woman literally scared to death by a spirit from her past.

Bava basically invented the cinematic version of *giallo* with *The Girl Who Knew Too Much* (1963), but his *Blood and Black Lace* (1964), which *Senses of Cinema* magazine calls "near abstraction on color and movement," crystallized it. *Blood and Black Lace* is a protopsychedelic nightmare in which a faceless killer (no, really—we see him/her many times, but he/she wears a featureless mask, trench coat, and hat) stalks and kills gorgeous models at an haute couture fashion house. Then, once *giallo* had grown in popularity, Bava blew it all apart with *Twitch of the Death Nerve*, a.k.a. *Bay of Blood* (1971). *Twitch* predicts *giallo*'s metamorphosis into the slasher movie by nearly a decade. Unlike earlier examples of *giallo*, *Twitch of the Death Nerve* does not focus on the hunt for the killer but rather on the graphic, bloody, borderline pornographic murders themselves. *Twitch*'s relentless stalk-and-slash violence appalled filmgoers, especially the "legitimate" art critics and highbrow types among whom Bava fandom had previously been fashionable. Bava lived to see his viewpoint vindicated by the "slasher" craze, but just barely; after making one last horror masterpiece (*Shock*, 1976), he died of a heart attack in 1980.

DARIO ARGENTO

Mario Bava may have invented the *giallo* genre, but Dario Argento is its most famous practitioner. This Italian director began his career with a series of twisted psychosexual detective stories that earned him the nickname "The Italian Hitchcock." Later in his career, he transitioned to films that combine the murder mysteries that had made him famous with supernatural horror, and the results are, to put it kindly, mixed. Some, like *Suspiria* (1977), are among the best horror movies ever made, and others...well, it's best to forget that Argento made much of anything in the '90s. He's still working today, but many (including your humble author) will tell you: if it was made after 1985, the year of *Phenomena* (starring a young Jennifer Connelly as a boarding school student whose communion with insects helps her catch a murderer), proceed with extreme caution.

Argento's movies are little concerned with reality, and as in *Kill Bill*, while his cinema worlds may bear a superficial resemblance to our own, they play by their own rules of surrealistic dream logic. He uses a refined aesthetic to present the most lurid of material, reflecting the commercial realities of the horror genre as well as his own background as an art critic. Because of this, and because the director's hand is so evident even in his weakest work (literally *and* figuratively—any time you see hands in black leather gloves reaching out to strangle or stab or whatever in an Argento flick, those are the director's mitts), critics tended to hold Argento in higher regard than most horror filmmakers. Of course this is all relative, as tearing horror flicks apart was practically a hobby for critics in the '70s, a practice that is thankfully going out of style.

Argento made the transition from art critic to artist by writing screenplays, and when Sergio Leone asked him to help write his spaghetti Western opus *Once Upon a Time in the West* (see chapter 8), this caught the eye of prominent producer Goffredo Lombardo, who commissioned him to write a *giallo*. This eventually became *The Bird with the Crystal Plumage* (1970), Argento's directorial debut. In *Bird*, he utilizes what would become his trademark gender-fuck flair in the story of a male foreigner who gets in over his head after witnessing a murder in an art gallery (another Argento staple) and then finding himself accused of the crime. *Bird* was the first of an excellent trilogy of "animal *giallos*"—the second being *Cat O' Nine Tails* (1971) and the third, the wonderfully titled *Four Flies on Grey Velvet* (1972)—featuring amateur dicks and shocking psychosexual twists.

He later made one of the greatest of all *giallos* with *Deep Red* (*Profondo Rosso*) (1975), which conjures up high-art influences such as art-film auteur Michelangelo Antonioni and the opera while still staying true to Argento's own excessive style. (You will see a lot of the title color in *Deep Red*. A whole lot.) *Deep Red* starts off as the tale of a psychic who uncovers an incestuous secret in the mind of an attendee at one of her seminars. The psychic is quickly and gruesomely murdered, which in turn is witnessed by Marc Daly (David Hemmings), an English musician living in Rome. As is de rigueur in an Argento movie, Marc becomes obsessed with learning the motivations behind the psychic's murder, an obsession that will lead him to some very dark places.

Deep Red hints at the supernatural, but those elements didn't really come forward in Argento's work until *Suspiria* (1977), Argento's masterpiece. *Suspiria* takes place at a magnificent German ballet school, where American Suzy Banyon (Jessica Harper, looking a bit like a Disney princess) arrives to begin her training just as students and staff begin getting bumped off in grisly and mysterious ways. *Suspiria* is very much a fairy tale, pitting a beautiful maiden against an evil witch, and as critic Lisa Schulte Sasse says about the movie: "In a conscious if ironic tribute to Disney, *Suspiria* is *about* intense color as much as it is *about* anything." Argento's use of color-coded lighting in *Suspiria* is incredible, as is the production design; he wanted to use actual children as the ballet students but had trouble financing a movie packed with glamorous scenes of little girls getting violently murdered, so he compromised by using adult actresses and just making all the sets about 50 percent bigger than normal.

Suspiria's fairy tale atmospherics contrast with the extreme cruelty of its murders. One victim falls into a storage area full of barbed wire where her terrified flailing just cuts her to ribbons. And in the opening scene, a woman is stalked and stabbed before her body is thrown through a stained glass skylight, Technicolor orange blood dripping onto the shards of colored glass as Goblin's iconic synth soundtrack reaches a fever pitch. The violence in *Suspiria* is brutal but abstract (and, I gotta say, scary as hell); it's a true example, like the *Female Prisoner Scorpion* series, of lurid material raised to the level of high art by an innovative director. *Suspiria* is the first of Argento's "Three Mothers" trilogy, about a family of powerful witches: there's Mater Suspiriorum, the Mother of Sighs, the oldest and wisest of the three; Mater Tenebrarum, the Mother of Darkness, the youngest and most cruel; and Mater Lachrymarum, the Mother of Tears, the most beautiful and powerful of them all. The second film in the trilogy, *Inferno* (1980), is stylish and satisfying, if not as inspired as *Suspiria*; but alas, its long-awaited completion, *Mother of Tears* (2007), is an unfortunate mess full of neogoth posturing that is for completists only.

LUCIO FULCI

Rather than blending high and low culture like his contemporary Dario Argento, Lucio Fulci goes straight for the reptile brain. The highly prolific Fulci spent much of his career as a journeyman director of bawdy sex comedies and postapocalyptic direct-to-video trash. He also made some significant entries into the *giallo* genre, but his best-known work doesn't follow the stalk-and-slash structure of most *giallo*s—hell, his *giallo*s don't follow the structure of most *giallo*s. What Fulci is famous for are hallucinatory, visceral gore films that use a nihilistic disgust for the human body to fuel a sickening sense of horror and unease. In other words, they don't just have blood and guts, they have sticky, goopy blood and steaming, slimy guts, with some punctured eyeballs thrown in for good measure.

An early classic, *Don't Torture a Duckling* (1972), is a delightfully perverse *giallo* that transgresses the taboos of religion (Fulci was violently anti-Catholic, and it shows) and pedophilia (a POV shot of two disembodied hands choking a young boy to death is way more sexual than it should be) for a depraved protoslasher about a murderer of children in the Italian countryside. Even better is *The Psychic* (a.k.a. *Seven Notes in Black*) (1977), which has so much subdued, shadowy *giallo* atmosphere that it's considered one of the best, even though its puzzle-piece plot is unusual for the genre. (It's unusual for Fulci, too—*The Psychic* plays more like an Argento film with a dash of Edgar Allen Poe than it does his other movies).

In the prologue to *The Psychic*, a woman commits suicide by jumping off of a cliff. Hundreds of miles away, her daughter instantly knows that her mother is dead—she's clairvoyant, you see. Fast-forward about fifteen, twenty years, and that girl has grown up into the alluring Virginia, played by Jennifer O'Neill. Virginia is driving on the highway when she has another of her psychic fits: what she sees are images of a woman trapped behind a wall, an older woman with blood on her head, a beautiful face on a magazine cover, a broken mirror, a lit cigarette, and a man limping in the dark. She is frightened. Her husband dismisses the visions, as do her psychiatrist and the police ... that is, until the discovery of a skeleton behind a brick wall in her husband's ancestral villa. *The Psychic* ends with a big twist and a killer last shot that will haunt you long after the movie's over, and the titular "seven notes" will be instantly recognizable to *Kill Bill* fans—it's the music that plays when The Bride wakes up from her coma and kills Buck!

Another of Fulci's most famous works is his "Gates of Hell" trilogy, three haunted-house movies (*City of the Living Dead* [1980], *The Beyond* [1981], and *The House by the Cemetery* [1981]) based on the idea of a—you guessed it—portal to hell opening up in a creepy old house. The best one is *The Beyond*, which starts off a haunted-house movie and ends up a zombie movie with an occult flair. It's the best distillation of Fulci's body-horror themes into one disjointed but compelling film full of symbolic imagery and bodies dissolving into a rainbow of fizzy goop. (Mostly the latter.) Katherine MacColl stars as Liza Merrill, a New York career girl who inherits a long-shuttered Victorian hotel just as her professional and personal life has hit a bit of a wall. It may seem like a lucky break, but this hotel is built on top of one of the seven Gateways to Hell, closed for decades but reopened by an inquisitive plumber looking for the source of a leak. That's going to hurt the property values!

But if you've seen one Fulci movie, you're probably seen *Zombie* (1979), also known as *Zombi 2*. George Romero's *Dawn of the Dead* (see chapter 6) had played well in Italy, where it was called *Zombi*; and so in a practice known as *figlia*, Fulci's unrelated movie about a cursed Caribbean island was marketed as a sequel. Despite this, *Zombie* is about as far from *Dawn of the Dead* as you can get while still having zombies. Romero was using them as instruments of social satire, but Fulci just wants to make you spew. His zombies are rotting from the inside out, oozing what looks like green Alka-Seltzer and slaughterhouse leftovers from the gaping holes where their stomachs used to be. All this gore might sound excessive, but it's actually extremely necessary—if it weren't for the disgust factor, you'd notice that these monsters move so sluggishly that the actors are clearly struggling to "run" slowly enough to get "caught." (Equally ludicrous is *Zombie*'s famous "Zombie vs. Shark" fight scene, featuring a clay-faced zombie slowly grappling with a sedated shark while a topless woman screams, but for some reason doesn't swim away, nearby.)

WU-TANG FOREVER:
A FIELD GUIDE TO THE WU-TANG CLAN

Thanks to their common obsession with kung fu movies, it was inevitable that Staten Island hip-hop collective The Wu-Tang Clan would someday join up with Tarantino. So it wasn't much of a surprise when Clan "Abbot" RZA was brought in to do some soundtrack work for *Kill Bill*, the first original music ever composed for a Tarantino movie. Kung fu is an essential part of the Clan's identity (they got their name from the movie *Shaolin and Wu Tang*), but RZA has always been especially fond of Hong Kong action. In 2012, he finished his own long-gestating kung fu epic, *The Man with the Iron Fists*, and on an episode of *MTV Cribs*, RZA described his bedroom thusly: "I be in here watching kung fu flicks and pornos." Nice.

The Wu-Tang Clan's structure revolutionized hip hop by allowing members to produce their own solo albums concurrently with "official" Clan albums, a policy that has led to only five Wu-Tang studio albums— *Enter the Wu-Tang (36 Chambers)* (1993), *Wu-Tang Forever* (1997), *The W* (2000), *Iron Flag* (2001), and *8 Diagrams* (2007)—but a dizzying array of solo work and guest spots from members of the Clan. These are the essentials:

RZA—RZA *as Bobby Digital in Stereo*
GZA/GENIUS—*Liquid Swords, Grandmasters* (with DJ Muggs)
METHOD MAN—*Tical*
RAEKWON—*Only Built 4 Cuban Linx, Only Built 4 Cuban Linx
. . . Part II*
GHOSTFACE KILLAH—*Supreme Clientele, The Pretty
Toney Album*
OL' DIRTY BASTARD—*Nigga Please*
INSPECTAH DECK—*Uncontrolled Substance*
MASTA KILLA—*No Said Date*

IL FANTASTICO VIAGGIO DEL GOBLIN

You may not think you know what Goblin sounds like, but you know what Goblin sounds like. Goblin is that eerie, hypnotic synthesizer music that, when you hear it in a movie, means that a zombie (or a demon, or maybe even a mad slasher) is slowly ambling in your general direction.

The interesting thing about Goblin is that although they're known almost exclusively as a "soundtrack band," they were together long before they scored their first film. They had already released an album under the name Cherry Five when Dario Argento called them in as replacements for the original composer of *Profondo Rosso* (1975), whom he had fired a few days before. They changed their name to Goblin to suit the movie's horror theme, and as they say in Italian, *il resto è storia*.

The partnership between Goblin and Argento proved extremely

fruitful, and for the next three years or so, Goblin churned out classic soundtrack after classic soundtrack, some of them quite commercially successful. But the band broke up for the first time after recording the *Dawn of the Dead* soundtrack and many times after that, shuffling around members so many times that by the early '80s, you couldn't rightly call any of their incarnations "Goblin" any more. Following a resurgence of interest in their sound, the original lineup re-formed in 2009; but alas, it was not to be, and after only a few live concerts, Goblin broke up yet again.

One upside of the contentious saga of Goblin is the new crop of musicians inspired by their style, so rather than lament the fact that the members of Goblin can't get past their own interpersonal demons, pop in Umberto's 2010 album *Prophecy of the Black Widow*, or Zombi's *Surface to Air* (2009) or *Escape Velocity* (2011), and pretend your bus is about to drive through a portal to hell or the guy sitting next to you is undergoing The Change.

ESSENTIAL GOBLIN

PROFONDO ROSSO (1975)
SUSPIRIA (1977)
ROLLER (1977)
ZOMBI (DAWN OF THE DEAD) (1978)

...or just pick up the excellent "Best of" collection *Fantastic Voyage of Goblin: The Sweet Sound of Hell* (Bella Casa Records) to get all the best tracks from these and more in one place.

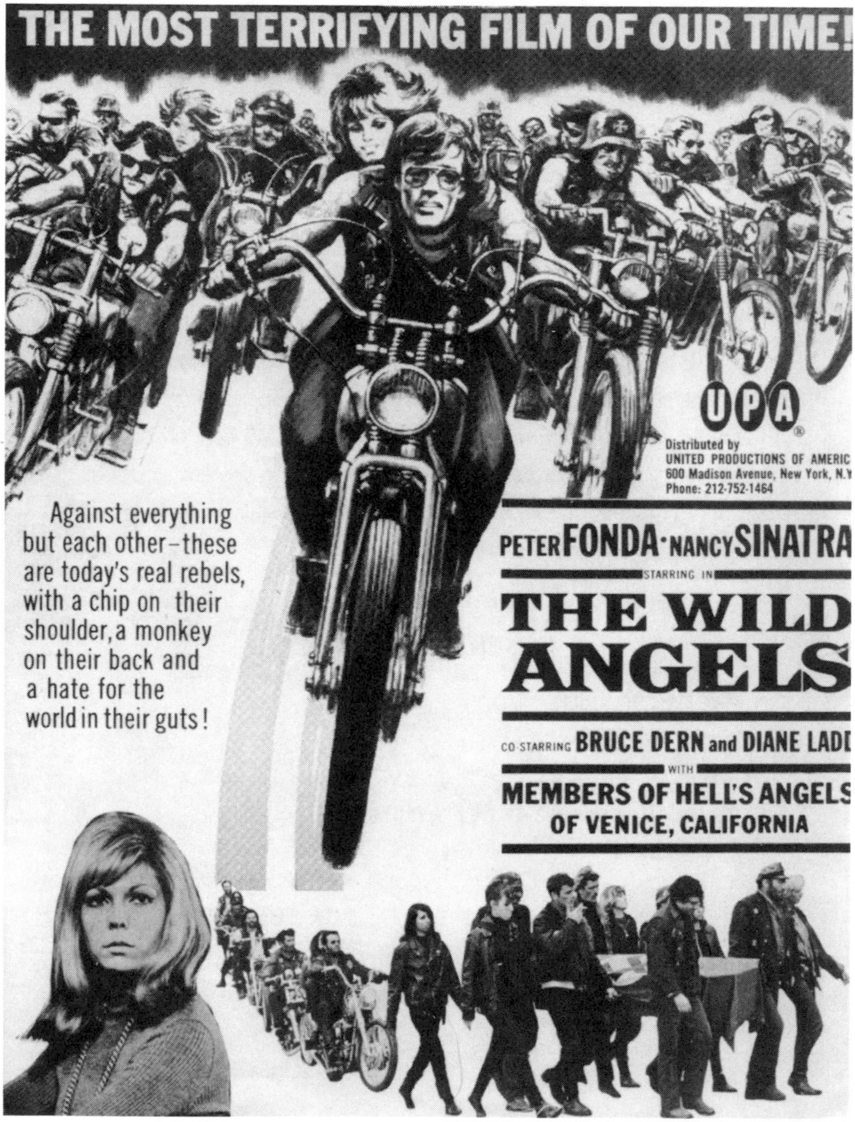

(American International Pictures/Photofest)

6

DEATH PROOF:
SHE-DEVILS ON WHEELS

I never use the term crap. Ever! These are not so-bad-they're-good movies. I love this stuff! And that's what we want to re-create. For lack of a better word, we want Grind House *to be a ride. I think we could both go out with our movies and have them stand on their own. But what's so good about this is it's two movies, and trailers, and bad prints, and if a little bit of gang violence breaks out in the theater, all the better! It just makes the whole experience more interactive!*
—QUENTIN TARANTINO, *Entertainment Weekly*
interview, June 2006

At the risk of sounding like a dictionary, technically speaking-ing, *grindhouse* and *exploitation* are not the same thing. A *grindhouse* (RIP) was a theater that never closed, and *exploitation* is the type of film they usually showed there. There are a lot of connotations surrounding the word *exploitation*, but all it really means is that in the absence of big stars and impressive production values, to sell a movie, you must have something to exploit. That thing is often sex or violence (usually a combination of the two), but it could be anything that draws attention, from the presence of real-life Hell's Angels to the shock value of Nazi imagery.

These types of movies are still around today. What else does a The Asylum flick such as *Battle of Los Angeles* have going for it but exploiting unwary Redbox customers who mistake it for *Battle: Los Angeles*? But now that major studios are willing to go places where once only hucksters dared to tread, many say exploitation's golden years have passed. Lest we get too nostalgic, remember that during the '60s and '70s, for every *Switchblade Sisters* or *The Texas Chainsaw Massacre*, there were a dozen shitty movies that the world has since (justly) forgotten. But the beauty of the exploitation system in that era was that as long as directors delivered the required amount of sex and violence, they were free to create the movie they wanted to create, which attracted young directors on the up and up as well as "jobbers" such as Jack Hill and Larry Cohen.

Exploitation has been around since the very beginning of the movies and has gone through many incarnations, from road shows featuring "educational presentations," mostly on sex ed, to drive-ins featuring all-night dusk-till-dawn trash-o-rama marathons. This history is well documented in books including *Grindhouse: The History of Adults Only Cinema* and documentaries such as *American Grindhouse* and *Schlock! The Secret History of American Movies.*

The specific exploitation milieu that Tarantino and Robert Rodriguez's movie *Grindhouse* is seeking to re-create, however, is the always unsanitary and sometimes downright terrifying movie-going experience of the inner-city grindhouse. The book *Sleazoid Express* does an excellent job of describing New York's 42nd Street back when Times Square was the world capital of cinematic sin, and when you stepped into one of those theaters, according to *Sleazoid*, you might encounter any combination of the following: junkies nodding off; decaying balconies full of gay hustlers; unspeakable fluids on the floors of the bathroom; pickpockets, masturbators, and all manner of violent and/or sexual acts to rival those on screen.

Obviously Tarantino and Rodriguez couldn't bus in switchblade-toting hustlers to every theater in America, but what they were able to re-create was the structure of a grindhouse show with a first feature, a second feature, and trailers in between. (They were also able to *approximate* the look of a grindhouse show with "scratches" and "missing reels," originally the result of wear and tear on the print from being passed through a projector twenty-four hours a day, but in this case accomplished with AfterEffects.)

Tarantino and Rodriguez had already been friends and collaborators for over a decade at this point, and whether *Grindhouse* originated with a poster Tarantino had hanging in his house or a double feature with trailers in between that he programmed for his friends depends on who and when you ask. Either way, the story goes that Rodriguez mentioned to Tarantino that he had always wanted to do a double feature, and Tarantino came up with the idea of calling it *Grindhouse* after the B-movie double features of his youth.

Tarantino's contribution to *Grindhouse* is *Death Proof,* and this time he tried a different, more deconstructionist approach, inspired by the book *Men, Women and Chainsaws* by Carol J. Clover, a feminist analysis of the slasher movie. In typically Tarantino fashion, the scope of his vision expanded beyond the slasher formula to include a badass gang of stuntwomen (including Zoe Bell, Uma Thurman's stunt double from *Kill Bill,* as herself) as living homages to the girl-gang genre. Then, he added an Alpine White 1970 Dodge Challenger in tribute to *Vanishing Point,* the ultimate example of the gearhead genre that also includes *Dirty Mary, Crazy Larry* and is the spiritual cousin of biker movies such as *The Savage Seven* and *Hell's Angels on Wheels.*

So brace yourself, because we've got rednecks in cars, rebels in cars, rebels on bikes, girls on bikes, girls with knives, guys with chainsaws, and nubile basketball players having sleepovers (and of course, the trailers, promising thrills that they know damn well they can't deliver), all part of the complex blend of ideas that went into *Death Proof,* and all with feet planted firmly to the sticky floor of the grindhouse.

SWITCHBLADE SISTERS

Jack Hill, whom you will remember from *Coffy* and *Foxy Brown* (if you don't, see chapter 3), is one of Tarantino's movie-making idols, and *Switchblade Sisters,* a.k.a. *The Jezebels* (1975), is his favorite Hill film. Tarantino calls Hill "the Howard Hawks of exploitation," because like the Hollywood master, Hill has done one of everything in the grindhouse universe, with his trademark wit and highly quotable dialogue running through them all like a delicious vein of chocolate in a gallon of Rocky Road. Tarantino likes Hill's entry into the "girl gang" genre so much, in fact, that he revived it and released it on his video label, Rolling Thunder Pictures. And thank goodness he did, because otherwise, we might never have gotten to see this delightfully rough, uncut diamond of a movie.

The thing with *Switchblade Sisters* (and all of Hill's work, really) is that you might start out thinking it's just a dumb, crappy movie that you can laugh at, but before long, you realize that you are laughing with the movie, not at it, and by the end, you're breathlessly rooting for the characters to succeed (or fail, as the case may be). So don't be put off by *Switchblade Sisters'* occasionally strident style and turn it off in the first five minutes, because you'll be missing out on one of the most outrageously entertaining movie-going experiences of your life. Yes, your life.

Switchblade Sisters updates the '60s aesthetic most people associate with "girl gangs" for the bell-bottomed, braless '70s. Our big-haired Jezebels are all minor sartorial miracles in black leather and denim, studded belts, and thigh-high boots, and they embody a refreshingly "real" range of body types. (For an even more radical approach to the girl gang, check out *She-Devils on Wheels*, a 1968 film by "Godfather of Gore" Herschell Gordon Lewis that isn't as good as *Sisters* but features real female bikers, some of whose looks you'd be hard pressed to find in any other movie, anywhere.) The most devastating style icon of them all is Patch (Monica Gayle), a lithe, catlike girl dressed in black, with long straight hair and a badass appliquéd eye patch.

Patch starts off as the #2 girl of the Dagger Debs, a gang of brawlin' lower-class white girls led by tomboyish gutter rat Lace (Robbie Lee) that specializes in shakedowns, petty theft, and swilling malt liquor. (The Dagger Debs are an offshoot of a similarly antiquated all-white boy gang, the Silver Daggers.) Our girls are hangin' tough with their fellas at a fast-food stand one afternoon when Lace spots what looks like fresh meat in Daisy Dukes and a Farrah hairdo. But what Lace doesn't know is that sweet young thing Maggie (Joanne Nail) ain't so sweet, and when the Debs try to hustle her out of her lunch money, she gives them a taste of her switchblade instead.

After the inevitable tussle—and yes, these bitches can brawl—the girls are all sent to the most cliché juvie of all time (complete with a butch lesbian guard named "Mom"), where Maggie continues to be a spitfire and gets her head dunked in a toilet for her trouble. Lace sees potential in Maggie's bad attitude, and it doesn't take long for her to become a full member of the Dagger Debs, replacing Patch as Lace's best friend and confidant. So Patch starts whispering poison about Maggie in Lace's ear, leading to some life-altering consequences for her and the rest of the Debs.

I won't tell you what comes next—you'll just have to see it for yourself—but I will tell you two things: First, someone makes a cake with the word *Jezebels* written on it in red icing, and second, thanks to her mysterious past, Maggie's got connections with an all-girl gang of Black Nationalist Maoists. And does this all-girl gang of Black Nationalist Maoists have their own tank? Of course they do. Are they going to drive it through the streets of Los Angeles? You bet your sweet ass they are, and you'd be wise to get out of their way.

FASTER, PUSSYCAT! KILL, KILL!

Call it high camp, call it low trash, just call *Faster, Pussycat! Kill, Kill!* (1965) "Russ Meyer's ode to the violence in women!" Russ Meyer was a leading sexploitation director and the inventor of the "nudie-cutie" film, a type of movie that used *very* loosely strung-together plot devices as an excuse to show topless women, and quickly disappeared, save for a few nostalgic curios, after the advent of XXX porn. (The first "nudie-cutie," Meyer's 1959 movie *The Immoral Mr. Teas*, is a quintessential example: A dental-supplies salesman receives a dose of laughing gas that allows him to see through women's clothes. Nudity ensues.) Most Meyer films of this period are disarmingly naive and even wholesome despite the nonstop parade of bare breasts, but you know from the opening moments that *Faster, Pussycat!* is going to be something different. The voiceover announcing "Ladies and Gentlemen, welcome to violence" may have something to do with it...

The "girls" in this "girl gang" are a trio of pneumatically blessed go-go dancers fixated on sex, speed, and savagery. Leading the pack is the pushy Varla (Tura Satana), a cigarillo-smoking alpha female ("more stallion than mare," one man calls her) who immediately dominates everyone she meets with her painted-on eyebrows and inconceivable cleavage. Backing her up are the surly, ambiguously foreign Rosie (Haji) and blonde, brash, beefcake-obsessed Bille (Lori Williams); together these three are an unstoppable force, a sort of Voltron of violence and overflowing bra cups whose screen presence overshadows every other aspect of the movie. Tura in particular (who, appropriately enough, started her career as an exotic dancer-cum-martial artist) exudes a domineering charisma that won her a loyal following of fans who were only too happy to worship at her feet until her death in 2011.

The first to taste the wrath of Varla and her girls are all-American boy Tommy (Ray Barlow) and his teenybopper girlfriend Linda (Susan Bernard), who have the misfortune of interrupting an afternoon of hot-rodding and cat fights out in the desert. Varla berates the boy until he agrees to race her, but during the rally, he loses control of the car. That's his first mistake. His second is insulting Varla, who, being the raging semi truck of a woman that she is, beats him to death and tells the gals "he's had a bad accident."

So the gang scoops up the terrified Linda and zooms off into the wastelands of inland California (Meyer was infamous for shooting with a tiny crew in remote locations, forcing his actresses to not only do their own hair and makeup but lug equipment too), leaving the "evidence" to rot in the desert sun. Not long afterward, they stop at a gas station, where they hear rumors of a wealthy old man (which perks up Varla's ears) and his big, dumb beefcake son (who's more Billie's speed) living on a nearby ranch. Intrigued, the gals head out to the ranch to try and get their hands on the cash using their kind of currency...honey. This all sounds very torrid, but in actuality, *Faster, Pussycat!* isn't as lurid as it seems. The violence is largely implied, and Meyer uses an unusually light hand with the nudity: those tops are a-heavin', but there's not a single bare breast in the entire flick (I know, *right?*)

Rumors have been going around for years that Tarantino is developing a remake of *Faster, Pussycat!*; the story even got as far as dubious casting news in 2008, when porn star Tera Patrick was supposedly being courted for the part of Varla. We'll see if it ever gets off the ground (I'm not so sure—remakes are more Robert Rodriguez's style), but there is a lot about *Faster, Pussycat!* that appeals to the director's sensibilities. Beyond the obvious protofeminist angle of a tough band of take-no-prisoners women that Tarantino paid homage to in *Death Proof, Faster, Pussycat!* is also full of witty dialogue, zingy one-liners, and innuendo thicker than a three-hundred-pound drag queen's ankles. And when Bille tells Varla, "Oh, you're cute, all right—like a velvet glove cast in iron!" it almost sounds like . . . well, whaddaya know …a line from a Tarantino movie.

THE WILD ANGELS/HELL'S ANGELS ON WHEELS

Prototypical biker flick *The Wild Angels* (1966) is almost worth it for Peter Fonda's rousing speech on the virtues of riding your machine without being hassled by The Man (seriously, look it up on YouTube), and Nancy Sinatra as a real down biker mama, but *Hell's Angels on Wheels* (1967), released the following year, is actually a better film. (This is not to say *Hell's Angels on Wheels* is without its flaws—like all biker films of its era, the movie makes extensive use of footage of Harleys roaring down the highway to pad its running time—but you know, relatively.)

Both films were made during the late '60s biker-movie boom, a period when producers rushed to exploit the burgeoning counterculture by applying it to an already-proven money-making formula—the "juvenile delinquent" movies that dominated drive-ins a decade before. This was way before the love affair between the Hell's Angels and the hippies came to a tragic end at Altamont, and since crime has always paid well at the box office, it was the former branch of antiestablishment rebels that these lovable cheats really latched onto. (Which is not to say the hippies didn't get their day on the exploitation circuit—1967's *The Trip* and *Riot on the Sunset Strip*, and 1968's *Wild in the Streets* and *Psych-Out*, all fall under the tattered rainbow banner of hippiesploitation.)

Shot on location in San Francisco, the unofficial capital of the '60s counterculture, *Hell's Angels on Wheels* features some very authentic-looking costumes, complete with full gang regalia, worn by some very authentic-looking extras. The credits boast the cooperation of the "Hell's Angels of Oakland, San Francisco, Daly City, Richmond and the Nomads of Sacramento," so it's safe to say that aside from our leads, those grubby, unshaven dudes you see harassing the good citizens of California are real outlaw bikers.

Adam Roarke starts alongside a young Jack Nicholson, who did his time on the B-movie circuit before getting his big break with a minor role in *Easy Rider* (1969), Hollywood's version of a counterculture movie. Nicholson plays "The Poet," a disaffected and pugilistic young gas-station attendant who hooks up with the Angels after helping them out in a nasty bar fight with a rival gang. Thus begins The Poet's journey toward full membership in the Hell's Angels, as he accompanies the gang to small-town Nevada for the orgy of sheep-chasing, wife-swapping, drunken punch-ups, and freaking out the squares that is known as a biker wedding. But when The Poet tries to "save" the boss's old lady, whom Buddy treats as little more than a piece of property to be passed around, things start to get complicated. Keep an eye out for an analogue of Hell's Angels fellow traveler Hunter S. Thompson, complete with cigarette holder and boater hat, body-painting the half-nude biker mamas in a beer- (and coke- and weed- and acid-) fueled party scene.

THE SAVAGE SEVEN

The Savage Seven (1968), like *Hell's Angels on Wheels*, was directed by Richard Rush and stars Adam Roarke, but it is much more obscure, possibly because there are no future Oscar winners in this one. However, it's a personal favorite of Tarantino's that played at the inaugural QT-Fest (see appendix 2). (Note that *The Savage Seven* is only available commercially on a very expensive out-of-print VHS, so if you see it for rent or on a DVD-R somewhere—grab it!)

Adam Roarke is once again a sensitive tough guy and leader of an outlaw motorcycle gang; his sidekicks John Garwood and

Richard Anders will also be familiar from *Hell's Angels on Wheels*. Max Julien—that's right, The Mack himself—also appears, as does grindhouse favorite Larry Bishop in one of his signature greaseball roles. (Bishop has a cameo as Bud's boss at the strip club in *Kill Bill: Volume 2*, and later directed an unfortunate mess of an outlaw biker movie called *Hell Ride* that was executive produced by Tarantino). The story concerns a gang of bikers rampaging, as bikers are wont to do, through an Indian reservation in the American Southwest. Led by Robert Walker Jr. as the blue-eyed Johnnie (Is he adopted? Was his father a Swede? Who knows?), the natives get caught up in a game of cowboys and Indians with the intruders, with the bikers as cowboys, and Indians as…uh…Indians.

The most interesting thing about *The Savage Seven* is its radical political subtext, which is very of its time; the movie posits that marginalized groups need to unite in common cause to take down the real enemy—The Man—who is pitting them against each other to tighten their grip on power. Overall, *The Savage Seven* is unjustly forgotten, as it's just as good as, if not better than, more widely available bikersploitation flicks of the era; the cinematography in particular is better than you'd expect, even on a cheap, unauthorized DVD. Director Richard Rush, something of a specialist in '60s counterculture movies, went on to do the also highly recommended *The Stunt Man* (1980), about a fugitive posing as a stunt man and an obsessive director who will do anything to get the shot.

VANISHING POINT

Did you ever see that show *Breaking Bad*? If not, *Breaking Bad* stars Bryan Cranston as a high school chemistry teacher who, after he is diagnosed with cancer, decides to leave behind an entire lifetime of doing what is expected of him and become a meth cook. On the show, they call this clean break from convention "Breaking Bad," but there are other terms for it—dropping out, going rogue, questioning authority, or simply not giving a fuck. However you want to put it, this total rejection of society is the theme of *Vanishing Point* (1971), an existential car-chase drama that is one of the greatest American movies of the 1970s.

Vanishing Point uses a speed freak named Kowalski and his Alpine White 1970 Dodge Challenger as stand-ins for the soul of America. See, Kowalski (Barry Newman) is a car-delivery-service driver who spends his time driving back and forth between cities out West. He's also a speed freak, in both the mechanical and the pharmaceutical sense. So Kowalski makes a bet with his dealer, a black outlaw biker, that he can get his newest delivery from Denver to San Francisco, usually a twenty-hour drive, in less than fifteen hours. That's it. That's the whole reason for Kowalski's high-speed assault on the American dream—a bet. But *Vanishing Point* doesn't dwell on this, and you shouldn't either, because the bet is simply a pretext for Kowalski's quest for total annihilation of the self, to finally become one with the asphalt under his wheels.

As Kowalski speeds across the desert, we discover that he's worn any number of macho hats in his day—a police officer, a stock-car driver, a Vietnam vet, a motocross racer—and he's been let down every single time. He also meets a variety of culturally loaded characters, such as a hippie snake-handling cult, a naked lady on a motorcycle, and a pair of gay hitchhikers, all of whom demonstrate that Kowalski isn't the only one looking to escape the past and lose himself on the open road. Providing the soundtrack to Kowalski's journey is Super Soul (Cleavon Little), a boisterous, blind African American DJ at the world's funkiest radio station, who wails and testifies and scans his police radio, giving guidance and encouragement to our (anti)hero and rallying the people around Kowalski's quest for supreme freedom. Thus spake Super Soul: "And there goes the Challenger, being chased by the blue, blue meanies on wheels. The vicious traffic squad cars are after our lone driver, the last American hero, the electric sitar, the demigod, the super driver of the golden West. But, it is written, if the evil spirit arms the tiger with claws, Brahman provideth wings for the dove."

Kowalski's brand new Alpine White 1970 Dodge Challenger R/T is a powerful machine and the real costar of the film, the roar of its engine dominating the soundtrack as it performs some really exceptional stunt driving. These were the days when there was no

CGI, and green screens sucked, so you had to do it all for real; and you can see plenty of local yokels standing by the side of the highway watching the stuntmen do their thing. (Director Richard Sarafian does a great job conveying a sense of acceleration, of perpetually moving forward, in ultrawide driving shots of the Challenger zooming across the wide-open stillness of the West.) Kowalski starts off small by breezing through a construction zone. Soon he's running a motorcycle cop off of the road, sparking a multistate race against the fuzz as he outdrives local sheriff after local sheriff before finally they send the helicopters after him...but outdriving a helicopter is nothing for a guy like Kowalski. I absolutely can't give away the ending, but I can tell you that the look on Kowalski's face as he drives toward his fate will stick with you for days afterward.

DIRTY MARY, CRAZY LARRY

What is *Dirty Mary, Crazy Larry* (1974)? Simply put, it's a chase movie. It's got car chases, motorcycle chases, helicopter chases . . . all manner of chases done in the authentic '70s style of *Vanishing Point*. This has made it a favorite of Tarantino's, who screened it alongside *The Savage Seven* at the inaugural QT-Fest.

Peter Fonda and Adam Roarke (with whom we are now quite well acquainted) star as Larry and Deke, two washed-up gearheads turned small-time hoods who rob a grocery store in hopes of raising some cash to jump-start their NASCAR ambitions. Unhappy with the take, they decide to hold the manager's wife and daughter hostage while they're at it. They get lucky, and the manager quickly ponies up the $150,000 ransom, but their luck runs out when, just as they're about to make off with the cash, Larry's one-night stand Mary (Susan George) shows up, and she is *pissed*. Determined that Larry will not love her and leave her, Mary forces her way into Larry and Deke's 1966 souped-up Chevy Impala, and this now-threesome takes off with an army of police vehicles on their heels.

Freewheeling and kooky, *Dirty Mary, Crazy Larry* has great rapport between introspective Deke; obnoxious, ditzy Mary; and gum-chewing nihilist Larry, who is superpissed that this chick is breaking his cool. They bicker and banter and don't really seem to like each other very much, but unlike *Vanishing Point*, the movie keeps it lighthearted and jokey, even as it wildly shifts between a heist flick, a road movie, and eventually a balls-out action extravaganza that Film School Rejects' J. L. Sosa describes as "a cargasm of destruction." You can see glimmers of *Dirty Mary, Crazy Larry*'s flippant approach to violence not only in *Death Proof* but in all of Tarantino's work, which shares with this movie the ability to move seamlessly between scenes of comedy and scenes of violence without disrupting the audience's engagement with the story.

THE TEXAS CHAINSAW MASSACRE

Halloween (1978) provided the template for all the slasher films that came in its wake, but you also can't underestimate the impact of *The Texas Chainsaw Massacre* (1974). Even if you've never seen *The Texas Chainsaw Massacre*, you probably know something about it ... and everything you know is probably wrong. It's the kind of movie people think is based on a true story (it's not), the kind of movie that people remember as being relentlessly gory (it's not), the kind of movie that inspires irrational superstitions about stopping at weird-looking gas stations off the side of the highway. That's how effective *The Texas Chainsaw Massacre* is.

Director Tobe Hooper is a native of the Texas hill country where the movie was shot, and through his camera, you can practically feel the heat and smell the fresh blood in the air. (All those dead animals and chunks of raw meat you see lying around? They're real, and really rotting in the hot Texas sun.) It's a grainy and occasionally poorly lit movie shot in a real down-and-dirty style (star Gunnar Hansen, a.k.a. Leatherface, says in the DVD commentary that he nearly killed both himself and actress Marilyn Burns for real on more than one occasion during the sleep-deprived shoot), but it all serves a purpose: to enhance the terrifying realness of it all.

It's also a major source of the "van full of kids stops off at a creepy gas station on their way to an isolated location where they will all surely be killed" cliché currently being deconstructed by movies such as *Cabin in the Woods* (2012). This particular group of youths— Sally (Burns); her whiny, wheelchair-bound brother, Franklin (Paul

A. Partain); her boyfriend, Jerry (Allen Danziger); her best friend, Pam (Teri McMinn); and Pam's boyfriend, Kirk (William Vail) — is bound for an abandoned house owned by Sally and Franklin's deceased grandparents. The first sign that they should probably just give up and go home is when they pick up a hitchhiker (Edwin Neal) who babbles incoherently about a slaughterhouse and slices his palm open with a knife ("It's a good knife," he says as the teens look on horrified and helpless) before pouncing on poor Franklin. But Sally is determined to go on, so they shove the nutcase out of the moving vehicle, stop at a gas station (which has no gas, another bad sign), wipe the blood off the van, and carry on toward their destination. When they get there, the able-bodied kids go off to explore, and leave Franklin alone in the house with the rats and the creepy chicken-bone talismans that ... somebody ... has built there. He's actually the lucky one—as he's sitting there pouting, his friends are being hung on meat hooks by a seriously twisted cannibal clan and their overweight, mentally deficient hulk of a butcher, Leatherface (Hansen), who wears a mask made of human skin. This is not to say that Franklin escapes unscathed, however...

There's a great moment when Kirk steps across the threshold of an isolated farmhouse; you know that *something* is going to happen soon, since you're halfway through *The Texas Chainsaw Massacre*, and it has been, thus far, chainsaw free. But still, when Leatherface lurches out to grab him and smashes him in the head with a sledgehammer, Kirk's leg twitching violently as he's dragged behind a heavy steel door, it's a shock. And when Leatherface slams that door shut, the tone of the movie totally changes. We go from what is clearly Texas into a claustrophobic underworld made of bones and skins and rotten dead flesh and the sounds of animals being slaughtered, added to the soundtrack to heighten the sense of unease. That's where the "massacre" comes in.

After the terrifying mindfuck of *The Texas Chainsaw Massacre*, Hooper made a couple more notable horror films (*Eaten Alive*, 1977, which opens with a familiar line: "My name is Buck, and I'm here to fuck," and the box-office hit *Poltergeist*, 1982) before deciding to spoof himself for the sequel, *The Texas Chainsaw Massacre 2* (1986).

The Texas Chainsaw Massacre 2 is goofy and self-referential where the original *Texas Chainsaw Massacre* is brutally realistic, but it does have a coked-up Dennis Hopper waving a chainsaw in each hand, which is worth the price of admission all by itself. There were more "Massacre" films made after *The Texas Chainsaw Massacre 2*, but after that...you're off the reservation, my friend. And if you've seen *The Texas Chainsaw Massacre*, you know not to wander too far. You never know what kind of weirdoes are out there.

MY BLOODY VALENTINE

My Bloody Valentine (1981) combines a popular cinematic trend (holiday-themed slasher movies) with a striking image (a miner in full uniform and gas mask) and some familiar genre tropes (horny young kids getting naked) to create a hybrid that for all of its sex and violence still seems rather quaint. This isn't really the movie's fault though: *My Bloody Valentine* was famously, extensively cut to avoid an X rating. Censors demanded cuts to every single kill scene in the movie, and the studios complied, spooked by the murder of John Lennon and the immense backlash that had accompanied *Friday the 13th* the year before.

Most of the time, these kinds of cuts are no big deal—a few frames that are barely perceptible when they do get restored. But with *My Bloody Valentine*, they really are two different movies; the cut version is practically bloodless, making all of the murder scenes short, vague, and confusing. It's a shame, too, because when you do see the deleted scenes, the deaths are creative (one victim is impaled on a shower head so the water sprays out of her open mouth) and the gore SFX are really quite well done. The uncut *My Bloody Valentine* remained unseen until 2009, when a re-release hit theaters in advance of a 3D remake. The restored version is still unavailable on Blu-ray; somewhat inexplicably, the distributor decided to include the extended gore sequences as special features rather than putting them back in the movie itself.

My Bloody Valentine is obviously not a Hollywood production (all the actors' Canadian accents are intact, director George Mihalka notes proudly). It was shot on location in the small mining town of Sydney Mines, Nova Scotia; the mine scenes were shot in a real coal mine that had been shut down only a few years before, and some rather drastic safety risks were taken by cast and crew alike. As Mihalka explains in a 2005 interview with the webzine *The Terror Trap*: "The only lighting equipment we were allowed to use was safety lighting equipment because there were no sparks. It was quite scary working like that because at a certain point, it becomes extremely dangerous. I mean, you can die. That's why they used to have canaries in coal mines."

The story is pretty straightforward, if a little silly: it's 1980, and the small town of Valentine Bluffs hasn't held a Valentine's Day dance in twenty years. You'd think they would, being the small town of Valentine's Bluffs and all, but this sleepy mining hamlet is afflicted with a curse. See, back in 1960, some mine foremen left their posts early to attend the Valentine's Day dance, resulting in a methane gas explosion that left a group of miners trapped underground for six weeks. The only survivor, Harry Warden, was driven insane by the ordeal and sent to a mental institution. He escaped exactly one year later to cut out the hearts of the guilty foremen, vowing that the same would happen to any unwary schmuck who ever celebrated Valentine's Day in Valentine's Bluffs again. But that was twenty years ago, and to a group of young miners, Harry Warden is nothing but a fairy tale. So the teens decide to defy the town sheriff and have a Valentine's Day party down at the mine. And as the audience already knows, this is one urban legend that's true ...

My Bloody Valentine is a giddy, somewhat guilty pleasure, but to its credit, unlike most slasher movies, it's carefully paced and structured well enough that you won't forget it right away. Tarantino hasn't, as he told *Entertainment Weekly* in 2006: "As far as slasher films go, of course, I love *Halloween* and all those. But as time's gone on, I think *My Bloody Valentine* may be my favorite."

SLUMBER PARTY MASSACRE

Slumber Party Massacre (1982) was conceived as a tongue-in-cheek feminist commentary on the slasher genre, a claim about which there can be no doubt when you consider the resume of screenwriter/ lesbian feminist icon Rita Mae Brown. *Slumber Party Massacre* was also directed by a woman, newbie director Amy Holden Jones. So how did it end up becoming just another orgy of gratuitous nudity and gore?

The exact reasons are somewhat obscure, but you can assume that Roger Corman, who required that a certain quota of bare breasts be included in every film that he produced, had something to do with it. Jones also says in a 2009 interview that she extensively modified the script before shooting began, changing it from a rather ham-handed parable on the dangers of sex (I mean, c'mon, the killer carries a *giant drill*) into an absurdly comic parable on the dangers of sex. Some of the bits Jones added are truly hilarious, like the pizza guy who arrives at the front door with his eyeballs drilled out ... "He's so cold," one of the girls says. "Is the pizza?" asks another.

Slumber Party Massacre opens with pretty, popular Trish (Michelle Michaels) getting ready for school, the camera lingering as she changes out of her nightie (of course). Later, after basketball practice, she invites her gal pals Kim (Debra Deliso), Jackie (Andree Honore), and Diane (Gina Hunter) over for a slumber party to celebrate her parents going away for the weekend. She also invites new-girl-in-town Val (Robin Stille, who you know from the first moment you see her is going to be the "final girl"), but after hearing Diane talking trash about her in the locker room, Val declines. In a thoroughly cinematic twist of fate, Val lives next door to Trish; having to hear the popular girls smoking pot and gossiping while you sit at home alone with your little sister seem like a high schooler's worst nightmare, but that's before escaped mental patient Russ Thorn (Michael Villella), better known as the "Driller Killer" (didja pick up on the Freudian subtext yet?), shows up to crash the party.

PIECES

Pieces (1982), on the other hand, is an especially nasty little slasher flick that comes to us by way of Spain and has absolutely no feminist subtext whatsoever. And while any semblance of quality writing or acting gets lost in the translation, the blood (real pig's blood procured from slaughterhouses by the way, none of that corn syrup and food coloring crap) certainly does not. *Pieces* comes armed with not one, but two, amazing taglines: "You don't have to go to Texas for a chainsaw massacre!" and "Pieces—it's exactly what you think it is!" The second one is actually a bit misleading, because no matter what you think you're in for when you sit down to watch *Pieces*, it's guaranteed to be so much more.

The effect is enhanced by the bizarre dubbing, but when you're watching *Pieces*, it's hard not to wonder if this is the work of a chemically imbalanced mind. Some of it is hilarious, like the random "kung fu professor" who wanders around punching and kicking at the air, but if you really think about them, some of the details are downright disturbing. Here's an example: One of the professors keeps the skull of a sixteen-year-old girl in his office. "It was a gift, I don't know where it came from," he says with a shrug. Sure, who doesn't get human skulls as gifts all the time? (He's supposed to be a professor of anatomy, so he has more reason to keep human skulls than most of us, but don't you think he would at least *wonder* where it came from?)

Pieces might be sick and twisted. That's one explanation. Another explanation is that it's just kind of dumb. Consider the rationale behind the whole thing: Forty years before in an idyllic New England town, a boy gets caught putting together a nudie puzzle by his horrified mother. The mother chastises the boy and takes away the puzzle, unwittingly unleashing a tidal wave of carnage as the boy goes berserk and chops his mother up into tiny pieces (Eh? *Ehhhh?*) This cunning little psychopath then hides in the bedroom closet and plays the traumatized victim when the police arrive. It's both wholly ridiculous and incredibly sick.

The remainder of *Pieces* pays like one of Patrick Bateman's masturbatory fantasies, a loosely connected tableau of topless chainsaw chases and surprise decapitations as a series of naughty, nubile, frequently nude co-eds get chopped into (say it with me now) pieces. In the end, *Pieces* lands on the side of "sick" rather than "silly" thanks to one horrifying anecdote: an actress actually wet her pants with fright while filming one of the murder scenes—you might too if a working chainsaw was mere inches from your torso—and *they left it in the movie.* And that, friends, is what *Pieces* is all about.

42ND STREET FOREVER

See! All the best parts of dozens of exploitation movies without having to sit through all of the bad dialogue and awkward acting!

Hear! The most overblown narration this side of the carnival midway!

Thrill! To boobs, bullets, beasts, and buckets upon buckets of blood!

There are a lot of exploitation trailer series out there, but accept no substitutes—*42nd Street Forever* is the best. Compiled by the exploitation experts at Synapse Films and coming in incarnations from the Alamo Drafthouse to XXX, *42nd Street Forever* covers every variety of schlock, from erotica to horror to sci-fi and action. Synapse released a Blu-ray combining the first two *42nd Street Forever* DVDs in May 2012; it contains a few titles that will be familiar from this book, but also adds some new selections, for a total of over three and a half hours of trailer heaven. Highlights include the trailer for *I Dismember Mama/ The Blood Spattered Bride*, featuring interviews with "moviegoers" driven mad by this depraved double feature; *The Italian Stallion*, a.k.a. Sylvester Stallone's porn debut from before he was famous; and a gimmicky warning for sensitive souls affected by "scalpel-slashing, arm-twisting, axe-hacking motorcycle maniacs" to close their eyes for the duration of the trailer for *The Undertaker and His Pals.* If you liked *Grindhouse*'s fake trailers, then this is the real deal.

DOUBLE DARE

Double Dare (2004) is a light and entertaining documentary on stuntwoman Zoe Bell and her mentor Jeannie Epper. It does touch on some of the gender politics of the stunt world—it's hard not to when telling Jeannie's story—but mostly it just celebrates Zoe and Jeannie and their fellow professional risk takers.

Zoe started out working as a stunt double for Lucy Lawless on the long-running TV series *Xena: Warrior Princess,* and she really shines through here (like she does in *Death Proof)* as charismatic, down-to-earth, and completely dedicated to her chosen profession. We first meet Zoe as *Xena* is about to film its final episode and follow her as she moves to Los Angeles to try to make it big. She goes in for training with Jeannie Epper, a legendary stunt woman who can really relate to the young adrenaline junkie—she stunt doubled for Lynda Carter for years on the TV show *Wonder Woman.* Jeannie is a real sweetheart and something of a den mother to the stunt community (a very Hollywood blend of teamsters and carnies), but she struggles for respect. Her male peers have long since been promoted to stunt coordinators and no longer have to take physical risks, but Jeannie is still being lit on fire for a living in her sixties.

A good half hour of the movie is dedicated to Zoe's experience being cast in and shooting *Kill Bill,* providing a fascinating glimpse behind the scenes from her audition to getting the call (thanks to a phone tap by the filmmakers) to a hilarious interview with Tarantino where he proclaims that until Zoe came on the scene, "we were shitting fucking bricks, man."

Zoe went on to double for the parts of Shoshanna and Bridget in *Inglourious Basterds* and has become an actress as well. (You might remember her from the Drew Barrymore roller derby movie *Whip It* [2009].) Her new project is the "female fight club" movie *Raze,* which began as a web series but is now being expanded into a feature film. Rachel Nichols (*P2, Star Trek*) costars in this blend of *Hostel* and *Gladiator* where women from all over the world are kidnapped and sent into an arena to fight to the death. *Raze*'s motto is "Fight or Die," and Zoe emphasizes that these ladies won't be fighting in high heels and leotards but tank tops and sweatpants, and make no mistake—they really could kick your ass.

WHEN THERE'S NO MORE ROOM IN HELL, IT'S TIME FOR SOME *PLANET TERROR* TRIPLE FEATURES

It feels like a John Carpenter movie that took place between Escape from New York *and* The Thing. *I wanted to do a zombie script a while back because there hadn't been any good zombie movies in a while. I got about 30 pages into it, and then all these zombie movies came out."*

—ROBERT RODRIGUEZ, *Entertainment Weekly* interview, 2006

Unlike Tarantino's deconstructionist take on the slasher movie in *Death Proof*, *Planet Terror* puts its influences proudly out front. Robert Rodriguez has been a fan of John Carpenter, the genre-movie master who made '80s classics such as *The Fog* (1981) and *The Thing* (1982), as well as the prototypical slasher movie *Halloween* (1978), since he was in junior high school. With *Planet Terror*, he pays loving tribute to Carpenter's style, down to the decidedly Carpenter-influenced score. So if you like *Planet Terror*, check out the triple feature of *They Live* (1988), *Escape from New York* (1981), and *Big Trouble in Little China (1986)*.

The style of *Planet Terror* may be John Carpenter's, but it's a zombie movie—er, excuse me, an "infected people" movie—through and through. We're currently at the tail end (thank God) of a new wave of painfully self-aware zombie movies, but if you like *Planet Terror*, this triple feature of zombie classics will be more up your alley:

First, put on *Dawn of the Dead* (1978). While it isn't really "jump out of your seat" scary, George Romero's satire of consumerism disguised as a zombie flick is one of the best horror movies ever made. It's got makeup by Tom Savini, Ken Fore as a shotgun-toting badass who calls people names like "flyboy," and hordes of zombies shuffling aimlessly around a suburban mall.

Next, pop in the Italo-horror schlock-fest *Nightmare City* (1980). Its story is the closest to *Planet Terror*'s out of the three—Hugo Stiglitz (a name that should ring a bell with *Inglourious Basterds* fans) stars as a reporter who happens to be on the scene when a mysterious disease that turns people into bloodthirsty monsters is unleashed. The infected rampage through an army base and eventually a hospital, each sporting a different level of "clay face," from a little schmear on the cheek to full makeup ... though the hands, mysteriously, remain unaffected.

And finally, you're going to need a palate cleanser after *Nightmare City*, so put on *The Return of the Living Dead* (1985), the very definition of a cinematic "romp." Like *Planet Terror*, in this one the sickness is spread by a gas—the experimental chemical weapon 2-4-5 Trioxin—but in *Return*, the gas doesn't affect the living, only the dead, which is bad news for the group of punks partying in the graveyard next door. *Return* revels in '80s excess, with all the nudity and gore the decade is famous for, and a totally righteous tagline: "They're back from the grave and ready to party!"

And to complete the unholy trinity, we've got the "Women in Prison" flicks briefly referenced in *Planet Terror* (it's the movie that the guards are watching on TV at the army base). Women in Prison movies are another staple of exploitation that has been in use practically since the silent era, but Rodriguez and Tarantino are especially fond of American International Pictures' series of Women in Prison flicks shot in the jungles of the Philippines.

For a crash course in AIP's take on the Women in Prison theme, first check out the documentary *Machete Maidens Unleashed!* (2012), which tells in detail the story of how producer Roger Corman discovered that it was much, much cheaper to shoot movies in the Philippines, where stunt men could be had for pennies a day and location permits were unheard of.

Then check out *The Big Bird Cage* (1971), directed by our old friend Jack Hill as a parody of his smash-hit Women in Prison flick *The Big Doll House* (1970), and starring Hill regulars Pam Grier and Sid Haig. Finally, top it all off with *Black Mama, White Mama* (1973), an all-girl, all-exploitation take on the Sidney Poitier movie The *Defiant Ones* (1958), starring Pam Grier and Margaret Markov as two feisty female prisoners, one black and one white, who escape from a hellish prison compound and flee through the jungle toward freedom. These two troublemakers don't get along, but if they're going to survive, they're going to have to stick together ... a task made easier by the shackles binding them at the wrist.

(Cambis Pictures/Photofest)

7

INGLOURIOUS BASTERDS:
FROM HELL TO VICTORY

Grindhouse **was a passion project for Tarantino, so as he** told *Sight and Sound* magazine in February 2008, he was "depressed" about its lackluster performance at the box office (though its eventual success on DVD must have cheered him up somewhat). But as he did with *Jackie Brown*, instead of moping over an experiment that failed, he just went back to what he knew. Tarantino had been working on *Inglourious Basterds* for quite some time before it finally became a reality in 2009; he talked about it as his "World War II epic" in interviews before *Kill Bill: Volume 1* came out in 2003, and the idea seems to have been brewing for a long, long time before that. Maybe even before he became a filmmaker—he joked with the *New York Times* in 2009, "The guys at Video Archives were like, 'Quentin, maybe one of these days you'll make your *Inglorious Bastards*.'"

As *Reservoir Dogs* is a heist movie without a heist, *Inglourious Basterds* is a war movie without a battle. It's more of an adventure movie set against the backdrop of a war, like the "bunch of guys on a mission" movies such as *The Dirty Dozen* (and its B-equivalent, the original *Inglorious Bastards*) that initially inspired the movie; though of course it wouldn't be a Tarantino movie unless he wove a few other story lines in there too. This time Tarantino includes a bit of a history lesson; in a 2009 *Huffington Post* interview with Kim Morgan, he talked at length about the German film industry before and during the Nazi era, describing propaganda minister Goebbels as a "studio mogul" and expressing his frustration with the idea that German cinema of the period began and ended with (violently anti-Semitic Nazi propaganda film) *Jud Suss*: "You know, here's the thing. I actually believe that when it comes to stuff like that, you should aim over the audience's head and let them reach out for it. If they have any interest in it, maybe they will now know who G. W. Pabst is now and maybe they'll investigate it."

Of course, as a history lesson you've got to take all this with a grain of salt, because unless you know absolutely nothing about World War II whatsoever, you know that things didn't turn out for Hitler like they do in the movie. Here *Inglourious Basterds* works as another one of Tarantino's favorite cinematic conventions: the revenge fantasy. He's using the idea of "alternative history" as a backdrop for a story that symbolically sets right what went so wrong in "history history," a story where the Jews aren't just victims of the Nazis but are out to collect their scalps, too.

THE DIRTY DOZEN

Quite a few big, expensive World War II epics came out in the '60s—*The Guns of Navarone, The Great Escape, The Longest Day,* and *Battle of Britain,* among others—and they all have a few things in common. They reassured vets that their war had been a just one and they had fought it well, they all did well at the box office as a result, they're all at least two and a half hours long, and they're all insufferably boring. Not so *The Dirty Dozen* (1967). Although it fits all but one of those criteria—it's a big, expensive, laudatory war picture made in a rather old-fashioned style—the difference with *The Dirty Dozen* is that it's got enough character to propel it through at least four hours of patriotic drivel.

A big part of *The Dirty Dozen*'s appeal is its all-star cast of '60s and '70s character actors: Lee Marvin, Charles Bronson, Telly Savalas, John Cassavetes, Jim Brown, and Donald Sutherland. A lot of rugged, weather-beaten countenances in that group, for sure, but the thing is that they were also people of substance who had actually seen and done things in their lives besides wait in their trailers for the next camera setup, and quite a few of them were World War II vets themselves. As Tarantino put it in a 2009 interview with *Time Out London*: "I think one of the things that's just amazing about 'The Dirty Dozen,' and why I don't think it could ever be duplicated today, is the fact that you could never find eight actors like that now. It was just a different breed of man."

In the same interview, Tarantino says that *Inglourious Basterds* started out as a straightforward "men on a mission" movie, a subgenre in which you're not gonna get any better than *The Dirty Dozen*. Lee Marvin stars as Major Reisman, a no-bullshit, plays-by-his-own-rules type of guy who has been handpicked by his commanding officers for a dangerous and top-secret mission. The reason they need a guy like Reisman is because the mission is to re-cruit twelve prisoners currently in military custody who have been "convicted and sentenced to death or long terms of imprisonment for murder, rape, robbery, and/or other crimes of violence and so forth." Reisman is then to take these convicts and relocate them to an isolated camp in the British countryside (Which one? The one that they'll build when they get there, naturally), where he will transform them from insubordinate criminals into an elite unit of soldiers. After that, they'll be sent on a classified mission deep be-hind enemy lines to…well, as Reisman is told, the exact nature of the mission "doesn't concern you now."

The Dirty Dozen spends the entirety of most movies—an hour and forty-one minutes, to be exact—depicting our "Dirty Dozen" (whose nickname comes from their hygiene, not their misbehavior) tussling and goofing off and all getting their chance to show us a little bit about themselves. The Dozen includes, among others, a certified psychopath (Cassavetes); a taciturn coal miner (Bronson); a mentally challenged murderer (Sutherland); a racist, misogynist sex offender (Savalas); and an African American soldier who *killed* a man who started some racist shit with him (Brown). By the last third of the film, we've come to love this ragtag band of stinky underdogs despite whatever crimes they may have committed in the past. (This, like all the more sordid implications of the film, is carefully glossed over; at one point Reisman buys his boys some hookers as a "graduation gift," and these violent criminals, who have gone months without sexual release…dance with them.) They have become a family, and so, after a dry run during a military exercise—which our Dozen win by cheating—Marvin sheds a proud tear. His boys are finally ready to grow up and start killing them some goddamned Nat-zies.

The mission turns out to be harshing the buzz of a chateau's worth of Nazi officers by busting into their party palace and raising some hell on the eve of D-day. Bronson—who speaks German— and Marvin lead the way, going undercover before the rest of the boys storm in and start busting some skulls. It's all in good fun ... until the very end of the film, when our heroes herd everyone at the chateau into the wine cellar and burn them all alive. It's totally unexpected, especially considering that other aspects of the film are downright hokey (I mean, do you remember the "dance" scene?), and Tarantino thinks it's one of the best parts of the movie: "I must say, that's an aspect that most people don't talk about with regard to *The Dirty Dozen*, and to me it's one of the strongest aspects of that film ...When you see that film now, you can't not see it: they create their own oven for the Nazis. And not just the Nazis: their wives, their girlfriends, all the collaborating-with-the-enemy bitches that are hanging out with them. They pile up those grenades and they douse them with gasoline, creating their own napalm, and they just burn 'em. [*Laughs.*] I mean, it's pretty fucked up!"

So if audiences were shocked in *Inglourious Basterds* by the wholesale murder of a room full of Germans, Nazi and civilian alike, they shouldn't have been. Tarantino was just quoting from a blockbuster movie from four decades before. And fucked up or not, this underdog tale was a huge moneymaker at the box office, even though Lee Marvin dismissed it as "crap." Oh, Lee. You were the best.

INGLORIOUS BASTARDS

The Italians do love reappropriating them some successful Hollywood formulas, and this particular *Dirty Dozen* rip-off comes courtesy of the prolific Enzo Castellari, who churned out thirty films in the spaghetti Western, postapocalyptic action, horror, crime, and macaroni combat (Italian B-movie war pictures) genres between 1968 and 1990. Castellari's not exactly what you would call an "auteur," but he does belong in the pantheon of B-movie directors who brought both consistent entertainment and the occasional moment of artistic vision to their work.

Tarantino says he saw *Inglorious Bastards* (1978) on TV when he was a kid and was very taken with the title—after all, how many times are you going to hear the word *bastard* on TV? For a while, he claims, he and his friends would refer to any "guys on a mission" movie as an "Inglorious Bastards" movie, thus providing a beautiful explanation for the title of his own World War II epic (though why he changed the spelling he's keeping to himself). Tarantino met Castellari when he started working on his own *Basterds* and eventually invited him out to LA for a special retrospective screening; they talk about all this and more in a special feature on the *Inglorious Bastards* DVD, and Castellari seems tickled pink by the whole thing.

As I mentioned before, the story is basically the same as *The Dirty Dozen*, with mustachioed Swedish-American actor and judo expert Bo Svenson stepping into the Lee Marvin role. All the major *Dirty Dozen* cast members get their B-equivalent: Fred Williamson takes over for Jim Brown as the African American soldier court-martialed for killing a racist officer (he takes over the Charles Bronson role as the second in command too); Peter Hooten for John Cassavettes as the convicted murderer; Michael Pergolani as the wild card, re-imagined from a sinister rapist into a goofy Italian pickpocket; and Jackie Basehart as the ...well, it kind of falls apart there, but Jackie rounds out the crew as a coward on trial for desertion.

After a Sergio Leone style (see chapter 8) opening credits sequence, this motley crew is herded onto a truck at an American prison camp. They're supposed to be transferred to a military jail, but fate has other plans; they're en route when Nazis attack the convoy and kill everyone except our titular Bastards, who seize the opportunity to steal a Jeep and get the fuck out of Dodge. Unable to return to their own side lest they be re-arrested or even executed, they head straight toward enemy lines in hopes of making it to neutral Switzerland. Eventually they meet up with the French

Resistance and find out that a group of Germans they killed earlier were actually American commandos; so in hopes of having their records cleared, they volunteer to take over the slain Americans' dangerous undercover mission.

Inglorious Bastards is a very picaresque movie, full of moments of irreverent comedy (though like *Inglourious Basterds*, it wouldn't be called a comedy per se) and lighthearted side adventures (the final mission doesn't get mentioned at all until the last forty-five minutes of the movie and isn't discussed in any detail until the last thirty). One memorable pit stop includes Nick's discovery of ten Aryan beauties bathing in their birthday suits in a woodland stream. The Bastards jump in to join them, but the arrival of Fred Williamson (going undercover as a white supremacist is tough for him, obviously) tips the girls off that these guys are not actually part of the Third Reich. So these naked Nazis grab their machine guns (hidden this whole time...where? Eh, doesn't matter) and start spraying bullets everywhere. Dirtier than *The Dirty Dozen*, indeed.

Speaking of Fred Williamson, interestingly, *Inglorious Bastards* was re-released in the '80s as a blaxploitation title, with most of Bo Svenson's role cut out so Williamson would appear to be the leader of the group. The title? *G.I. Bro.* Unfortunately *G.I. Bro* is extremely out of print, but you can get *Inglorious Bastards* on a nice double-DVD set from Severin Films, which re-released some seminal macaroni combat titles after the success of *Inglourious Basterds* in 2009.

BATTLE SQUADRON, A.K.A. EAGLES OVER LONDON

One of those Severin re-releases is *Battle Squadron*, a.k.a. *Eagles Over London* (1969), another Castellari creation that came out nine years before the original *Inglorious Bastards*. Castellari had only a few cheaply produced spaghetti Westerns under his belt when he directed *Battle Squadron*, but it is the premiere film in the macaroni combat canon, thanks to his ingenious visual flair, a large cast of international all-stars, and a larger-than-usual budget spent wisely onscreen.

Castellari does great work in *Battle Squadron*, but he wasn't the producers' original choice for the job. He was hired as a second unit director to do special-effects footage, and when he was asked to do a split-screen sequence, he had never even *heard* of the technique. But Castellari is a quick study, and after watching a couple of American movies that used split-screen, he shot some really cool triple split-screen sequences. The producers were so impressed that they asked him to direct the entire film. Castellari comes up with some exciting uses of lighting (a love scene lit by the explosions of an air raid outside), movement (the camera spinning around in a dizzying circle as a character is betrayed and killed), and creative camera angles (at one point, we see a battle through the perspective of a bullet hole in a helmet). But while Castellari's going above and beyond, *Battle Squadron* is a B-movie at heart, fixated on big explosions, pretty ladies, and lots of noisy action.

The story hinges on a British captain's efforts to root out a group of nefarious Nazi spies who infiltrated British forces during the evacuation of Dunkirk. (You'll just have to suspend your disbelief here, because pretty much everybody, British and German alike, is actually Italian, and the rolling hills of Dover are clearly the scrub-covered foothills of Rome.) Their mission is to disable the Brits' high-tech radar system so the Luftwaffe can unleash a devastating series of bombings and cripple the English infrastructure. After the British find out about this iniquitous plan, the focus shifts to British Captain Paul Stevens (Frederick Stafford), who with the aid of Air Marshal George Taylor (Van Johnson) foils the Nazis' plan. Oh, and this is not in any way based on a true story, despite all the stock footage and canned Churchill speeches.

Large portions of the action scenes in *Battle Squadron* (Castellari guesses about 30 percent) were lifted wholesale and spliced into the also famous, but not as good (partially because it's 30 percent composed of another movie) 1979 macaroni combat movie *From Hell to Victory*, directed by Umberto Lenzi. Apparently Castellari was completely unaware that such recycling was going on until he saw *From Hell to Victory* in the theater, a betrayal that he was angry about for quite some time.

OPERATION CROSSBOW

Operation Crossbow (1965) is a very, very—or should I say *veddy, veddy*—British spy film in the James Bond mold. Hinging on the moneymaking combination of the mid-'60s spy craze and nostalgia for the "Great War," *Operation Crossbow* tracks three Allied agents' efforts to stop the Nazis from developing The Big One by going undercover in a top-secret rocket propulsion lab. Like *Inglourious Basterds, Operation Crossbow* is not a "war movie" per se, but a thriller set against the backdrop of a war; it's less of a tank rolling over the hills of Normandy than a tightly wound pocket watch with many small, moving parts. (Also like *Inglourious Basterds,* in *Operation Crossbow* the Germans speak subtitled German and the French subtitled French, with English used only when it fits the context of the movie. It's a nice touch: using German-accented English is so *lazy.*)

Sophia Loren is given top billing, presumably because she's at her gap-toothed sexiest here (and, uh, also because her husband produced the movie). It's definitely not because of her extensive screen time. *Operation Crossbow* actually has quite a large cast, with several interconnected story lines going on in different places at once. Tying the whole thing together are British intelligence official Duncan Sandys (Richard Johnson), who has been sent on orders of his father-in-law Winston Churchill to investigate rumors of a German "secret weapon"; and chief science official Professor Lindemann (Trevor Howard), who dismisses these rumors as pure fantasy. The Germans don't have the know-how to build a rocket, Lindemann says. But in fact they do, thanks to aviatrix Hannah Reitsch (Barbara Rütting), a test pilot and Hitler's personal aerialist, whose innovations allow the Nazis to begin mass producing the V-1 flying bomb in secret underground factories.

Before long, V-1s begin to fall on London, leading to the most bittersweet "told you so" of all time by Sandys to Lindemann and then a nationwide manhunt for engineers who can double as spies. The three men ultimately selected are Robert Henshaw (Tom Courtenay), Phil Bradley (Jeremy Kemp), and US Air Force Lieutenant John Curtis (George Peppard). These three are then given the identities of recently deceased foreign collaborators and sent out to work in the Nazi's top-secret labs. Complications ensue when Nora (ah, *there's* Sophia Loren), the estranged wife of one of the dead men, comes looking for him to sign custody papers for their kids. This is just the beginning of the engrossing and entertaining story of *Operation Crossbow*, which unlike *Battle Squadron* is based on a true story.

CROSS OF IRON

Sam Peckinpah was always an iconoclast. His "anti-Western" *The Wild Bunch* (1969) sparked a national uproar for its graphic violence and morally ambiguous characters, and his later films *Straw Dogs* (1971) and *Bring Me the Head of Alfredo Garcia* (1974) were condemned by critics as the work of a warped and sadistic mind. So when Peckinpah finally got around to making his World War II epic *Cross of Iron* in 1977, it should have surprised no one that he chose to tell the story from a German perspective.

Cross of Iron centers around the class conflict between hardened veteran Corporal Steiner (James Coburn) and aristocratic pretty-boy Captain Stransky (Maximillian Schell), who, to be fair, does his best to make *everyone* hate him by declaring he requested a transfer from occupied France to the Russian front so he could get back at his wealthy daddy. That's not the best way to make friends with a bunch of battle-weary draftees who just want to go home, dude. Anyway, Steiner's distrust of this perfumed blue blood is proven correct when Stransky takes credit for a successful counterattack against the Russians that the entire unit knows was actually led by a lieutenant killed in battle.

By the time *Cross of Iron* began shooting, Peckinpah's once-legendary attention to detail had begun to slip, and with the dual handicaps of a shoestring budget and his raging alcoholism, the production seemed doomed to failure. But before running out of money, Peckinpah managed to shoot a series of brutally realistic battle scenes. He used real Soviet tanks, real German submachine guns, and some of the most gorgeous gore effects ever seen on film, pairing them without a hint of irony with a bleak and nihilistic antiwar message.

Cross of Iron had the misfortune of debuting in theaters alongside the box-office phenomenon *Star Wars*; one of the few people who actually went to see it was Tarantino, who told *Time Out London* in 2009 that he walked for three hours across Los Angeles to get to the only theater that was playing it: "I was a little boy, I didn't know anything about the Russian front, so I guess it went over my head," he said. "I learned to appreciate it later." As did everyone else: although *Cross of Iron* failed to make much of an impact outside of Germany, where it was the biggest box-office hit since *The Sound of Music*, its reputation has grown considerably over the years, and it now regularly sits alongside films such as *Saving Private Ryan* and *The Thin Red Line* as one of the greatest war movies of all time.

ILSA, SHE WOLF OF THE SS

Rare is the movie that makes you feel like kind of a bad person just for *recommending* it, and *Ilsa, She Wolf of the SS* (1975) is in that elite group. But if you can forget everything you've ever heard about political correctness and just wallow in the depravity like the proverbial pig in shit for an hour and a half, you may find yourself—horrors!—*enjoying* it.

Ilsa's fearsome reputation comes courtesy of its questionably tasteful yet undeniably titillating commingling of Nazi medical experimentation and sadomasochistic sexuality, brought to you courtesy of master sleaze merchant David F. Friedman, here to ensure that the nudity is extra gratuitous (practically all of the female characters appear nude at some point) and the gore is extra gory (topless whippings, topless pressure-chamber torture, topless electrified dildo torture, and on and on and on). Friedman, bless him, was an honest-to-god carny who produced fifty-six morally dubious B-pictures in his long and gloriously undistinguished career, but the *Ilsa* films were his crowning achievement. (Director Don Edmonds wasn't so proud of his role in the film: "the total whore in me came out," he said in an interview for the documentary *American Grindhouse*.)

Ilsa, She Wolf of the SS features what may be the most insincere title card of all time: "The producers dedicate this film with the hope that these heinous crimes will never occur again." Crocodile tears shed, Friedman and Edmonds then proceed to show you nothing *but* those crimes, committed at the hand of busty blonde ice queen Dyanne Thorne. Thorne started her career as a showgirl before appearing in all manner of sexploitation pictures, and is now a registered minister who conducts weddings in Las Vegas. But don't worry, Dyanne fans, your unrepentant bitch goddess hasn't mellowed in her old age. She said in a 2007 interview about *Ilsa* that "the script was trash, but the character seduced me ... I totally respect where my critics are coming from, but people need to lighten up."

Thorne's character, Ilsa Koch, is *verrrrrry* loosely based on a real-life Nazi war criminal named Ilse Koch, also known as "The Witch of Buchenwald"; the real Ilse was the wife of concentration camp *kommandant* Karl-Otto Koch, whose crimes against humanity included turning prisoners with interesting tattoos into human-skin lampshades. Our Ilsa's skin fixation is of a far lustier nature, however, and when she hand-picks male prisoners from the barracks of *her* Nazi death camp, she's looking for a breeding stud, not a skin to hang on her wall. (The women Ilsa plucks from the camp face a more gruesome fate—she chooses the bustiest of them, all played by famous nudie models such as Uschi Digard and Sharon Kelly, to act as guinea pigs and prove her pet theory that women can endure torture better than men.) After taking these unlucky studs for a ride, if they fail to satisfy her—and you should not be surprised that she's insatiable—she castrates them for the crime of going soft. Not one knob has survived a night with Ilsa ...not yet, anyway.

Enter German American stud Wolfe (Gregory Knoph), a prisoner of war who possesses the porn star–like ability to delay ejaculation indefinitely. Wolfe is the first man to ever sexually satisfy Ilsa, and seeing an opportunity to screw the sense right out of the lady *kommandant's* head, he begins fomenting a rebellion against Ilsa's reign of sexual terror while keeping her distracted with frequent bratwurst injections. All this coincides with the visit of a cartoonishly German general played by Richard Kennedy, as Wolfgang Rohem. In one of the film's sickest sequences, Ilsa greets the general with a "surprise" of a naked female prisoner standing on top of a block of ice, razor wire tied loosely around her neck; when the ice melts and her feet slip, she will be immediately decapitated. The General thinks this is just hilarious, and is so pleased with Ilsa that he asks her to piss on him. Being a good soldier of the Third Reich, she obliges. (Everyone in the movie does an admirable job of playing it straight, even though they're filming a soft-core porno on the set of *Hogan's Heroes*.)

Thorne cuts an imposing figure as Ilsa, and dressed in shiny black boots, a Waffen SS hat, and a crisp white button-down shirt that frames her heaving cleavage, the boner factor for the masochistic male is quite obvious. Those same boners propelled *Ilsa* to a six-month run at the Apollo Theater on 42nd Street, then the sleaze capital of the world, and three sequels of diminishing quality: *Ilsa, Harem Keeper of the Oil Sheiks* (1976); *Wanda, the Wicked Warden* (a.k.a. *Ilsa, the Wicked Warden*) (1977); and *Ilsa, Tigress of Siberia* (1977). But underneath all the taboo sexuality, Thorne is just a cartoon girl playing a cartoon part, and while she may be artless, she's also guileless. And when you look at her that way, she's actually kind of ...cute.

BLACK BOOK

By 2006, Paul Verhoeven was in dire need of a comeback. He had left his native Netherlands in the '80s for the greener pastures and bigger budgets of America, where he had reached the peak of Hollywood success with a series of smashes including *Robocop* (1987), *Total Recall* (1990), and *Basic Instinct* (1992), only to blow it all with the infamous NC-17 box-office bomb *Showgirls* (1995). (I actually really *like Showgirls*, but that's a story for another time.) Verhoeven then churned out a couple more limp flicks like *Starship Troopers* (1997), but his Hollywood career never really recovered. By the early 2000s, he had returned to Europe with his tail between his legs, but rather than give up, Verhoeven got back together with his old screenwriting partner Gerard Soeteman and restarted his World War II epic *Black Book*. (Like *Inglourious Basterds*, *Black Book* was a long time coming. Verhoeven and Soeteman worked on it off and on for fifteen years before finally finishing the script.) And what a comeback! *Black Book* was a huge commercial and critical success in Europe and launched a new chapter in Verhoeven's career; now he's got another historical drama in the works called *Hidden Force*, starring Dutch actors and being paid for with Dutch money. Eat it, Hollywood!

Set at the tail end of World War II, with action continuing long into the post-war period, *Black Book*'s story is gripping, provocative, and most importantly, one you haven't heard a million times before—and Verhoeven insists that it's all based on historical fact. *Black Book* focuses on the collaborators, the cowards, and the anti-Semites who flourished in the Netherlands under Nazi occupation, and it's not afraid to get rough in terms of violence, sex, and gratuitous nudity (but what would you expect from the guy who brought you *Basic Instinct?*) In *Black Book*, the "heroes" have malicious intentions and the "villains" are just trying to do the best that they can under the circumstances. Things are not as they seem, and if a Nazi can be a hero, then a freedom fighter can be a villain. As Verhoeven told the UK's *Guardian* newspaper in 2006: "In this movie, everything has a shade of grey. There are no people who are completely good and no people who are completely bad. It's like life. It's not very Hollywoodian."

Our one true heroine is the beautiful and talented Jewish nightclub singer Rachel Stein, a.k.a. Ellis de Vries (Carice Van Houten). Rachel is in hiding in the Dutch countryside, but when her hiding place is destroyed in an air raid, she is forced to flee for her life. After an act of betrayal leads to a deadly encounter with the Nazis, Rachel joins the Dutch resistance and is given a most dangerous assignment: go undercover in the heart of German power by seducing Nazi intelligence officer Ludwig Müntze (Sebastian Koch). Before her trials are over, Rachel's wit and bravery will be pushed to their limits as enemies on all sides try to take her down. But Rachel is a survivor. Van Houten went through some intense shit (even literally at one point) to play Rachel, and she is to be commended both for the strength of her performance and her bravery in agreeing to do this stuff at all. She does everything in this movie: action scenes in high heels and an evening gown;

graphic nudity (much has been made about the scene where she dyes her pubes); and most terrifying of all, live singing.

ROLLING THUNDER

Rolling Thunder (1977) is a movie that is both very much of its time and still relevant today. A favorite of Tarantino's (he named his video label Rolling Thunder Pictures after it), *Rolling Thunder* was cowritten by Paul Schrader, who also wrote the screenplay for *Taxi Driver*. And while it's not *quite* as good as Martin Scorsese's film, it has a similar gritty, realistic feel. *Rolling Thunder* is a microcosm of the spiritual crisis facing the United States at the end of the Vietnam War, when thousands of soldiers returned home to face ambivalence at best and outright hostility at worst. When help was offered at all, it was as empty a gesture as a briefcase of silver dollars (you'll see), and many disabled vets were abandoned and left to live on the streets. Charles Rane, the main character of *Rolling Thunder*, personifies America's guilty conscience on the issue, and he's out to get some revenge.

Major Charles Rane (William Devane) comes home to San Antonio, Texas, after several years in a Vietnamese prison camp with his war buddy Sergeant First Class Johnny Vohden (a young Tommy Lee Jones). They're given a hero's welcome by the patriotic, aggressively wholesome crowd that has come to greet them with hand-drawn signs and John Phillip Souza marches, but we know from the beginning that something is amiss. Rane is given the keys to a brand-new Cadillac and $2,555 in silver dollars—one for every day he spent in the "Hanoi Hilton" plus "one for good luck"—but what does he have to show for all those years of hell, *really*? He's been gone for a long time, so long his wife assumed he was dead and got engaged to another man; so long that his son, a boy of eight who was eighteen months old when his father left for war, doesn't remember him at all. On top of all that, he's been suffering from PTSD symptoms, but this is before anyone outside of the military took PTSD seriously, and Vohden is the only one who sympathizes.

So when some local yokels come to relieve Rane of his silver dollars, it doesn't take much for him to snap back into battle mode. These particular bullies go way beyond a simple beating, sticking

Rane's hand into a garbage disposal when he refuses to talk and murdering his wife and son in cold blood for witnessing it. What those thugs don't realize, however, is that they are fucking with exactly the wrong guy. Rane makes himself a sharpened hook for a hand and sets about doing the only thing he knows how to do anymore—raining the wrath of God down on the men who have wronged him. Joining him in his vendetta are Vohden and beauty queen Linda Forchet (Linda Haynes), a self-described "groupie" who wore Rane's ID bracelet the entire time he was away.

Rolling Thunder is a vastly underrated film that has never gotten a proper DVD release, but it is available in a decent VHS-quality transfer directly from the Warner Brothers Archives. It's just one of an entire cycle of Vietnam-vet revenge movies: check out *The Exterminator* (1980) for the 42nd Street equivalent; *Billy Jack* (1971) for the lefty Native-American-pride angle; *First Blood* (1982) (the original "Rambo" movie) for the Hollywood fantasy; and *Combat Shock* (1986) for the disturbing, twisted art film. The pissed-off Vietnam vet with a chip on his shoulder petered out as a plot device sometime in the mid-'80s, but now that we're in a similarly ugly late-period phase of the "War on Terror," it's high time to revisit the genre.

THREE KINGS

There haven't really been any great movies made about the (second) Iraq war (*The Hurt Locker* and *Restrepo* are about Afghanistan, remember), probably because we, as a nation, haven't had time to properly process it yet. After all, most of the good movies about Vietnam and World War II were made *after* the wars had ended, and the best of those were made by people who experienced those conflicts firsthand. *Three Kings* (1999) breaks the Iraq curve in a couple of ways, though; first of all, it's one of a relatively small handful of movies to deal with the first Iraq war, a.k.a. Operation Desert Storm, and secondly, it's not really *about* the war at all. It's a stylish black comedy about a gold heist that takes place during the Persian Gulf conflict.

Operation Desert Storm is drawing to a close, and there among the confusion are Major Archie Gates (George Clooney), a career soldier on the brink of retirement; new father Sergeant Troy Barlow

(Mark Wahlberg); and Chief Elgin (Ice Cube), an average soldier who's not especially looking forward to going back to Detroit. When one of the trio finds a map pointing to a cache of stolen Kuwaiti gold, these "Three Kings," disillusioned with their role as liberators, decide to take a piece of the action for themselves. All this war bullshit ought to be good for *something*, right? But as they strike out on their own and head deeper and deeper into the chaos, Gates, Barlow, and Elgin realize what they are really leaving behind. The Americans promised support to the Iraqis if they joined the fight against Saddam, and now the US has given them . . . what? Anarchy and massive loss of life, that's what, and to make things worse, they didn't even topple Saddam. This isn't to say that *Three Kings* is a serious "issues" film though. It's not; it's just a sharply observed one, an irreverent and zippy take on the war movie and the foolishness of the American "mission" in Iraq.

BRIAN DEPALMA

Like all of Tarantino's films, *Inglourious Basterds* is a mad hodge-podge of influences. But one that comes forward more clearly in *Basterds* than in any of his other films (so far, anyway) is the influence of one of Tarantino's movie-making heroes: Brian DePalma. As a budding young filmmaker, Tarantino even kept a scrapbook of newspaper articles about De Palma's films.

Tarantino is a passionate fan of DePalma's 1981 thriller *Blow Out*, starring John Travolta as a movie sound technician who accidentally records an assassination while shooting a slasher flick. (In fact, Tarantino's love for that movie factored into the decision to cast Travolta in *Pulp Fiction*.) Shades of *Blow Out* can be seen in the climactic projection-room sequences of *Inglorious Basterds*, and the scene where Shoshanna dresses for the *Nation's Pride* premiere to the tune of David Bowie's "Cat People (Putting Out Fire)" also pays homage to De Palma's slick, luxurious style.

Like Tarantino, DePalma is known for reinterpreting influences from his favorite movies, but with DePalma there's really only one filmmaker you need to know: Alfred Hitchcock. Brian DePalma loooooooves Hitchcock, and it shows. He's made several commercially successful films in his career (*Carrie* [1976], *Scarface* [1983], *Mission: Impossible* [1996]), but the quintessential DePalma is the macabre master of neo-noir thrillers. Also like Tarantino, De Palma inspires extreme reactions in cinephiles; either you love DePalma and think he's an underrated genius, or you cover your ears and go "gaahhhh" at the very mention of his name. Part of the reason is the complicated sexual politics of his thrillers. They all display a morbid fixation on death as a kind of impotence, a sentiment reflected in recurring themes of voyeurism, transgendered killers, and the decadent sexuality of the femme fatale.

Brian DePalma
Selected Filmography

SISTERS (1973)

DRESSED TO KILL (1980)

BLOW OUT (1981)

BODY DOUBLE (1984)

CARLITO'S WAY (1997)

ELI ROTH

A side from Robert Rodriguez, the other name you'll hear a lot in "Quentin Tarantino and ____ Present" is Eli Roth, the Boston-born film director whom many people know best as "The Bear Jew" in *Inglourious Basterds*. Roth hasn't done that many movies in his career, but he's been involved in many more, usually in some capacity with his friend and mentor Tarantino. Like Rodriguez, Roth grew up making amateur Super 8 films, and he describes his young self as a complete and utter horror nerd; he claims that at his Bar Mitzvah, he had a blood-spatter cake and "sawed" himself in half with a "chainsaw" in front of his assembled friends and family. (Nice!) He went on to attend NYU's famous film school, where his thesis film, *Restaurant Dogs*, won a student Academy Award, despite being dismissed by his professors as "sophomoric, overtly offensive, and gratuitously violent."

Roth then worked an assortment of thankless crew jobs for nearly a decade while trying to get his screenplay *Cabin Fever* financed; finally completed in 2002, *Cabin Fever* is an affectionate tribute to '70s horror movies such as *The Evil Dead* that alternately satirizes and wallows in the conventions of a brainless horror flick. *Cabin Fever* sparked a bidding war at the Toronto Film Festival and attracted the attention of Tarantino, who told *New York* magazine: "He's what horror films have been waiting for: not a video director trying to make his first movie and then move on or the older guy who resents the fact that he's still doing horror films. Eli wants to make horror films."

Tarantino had long been one of Roth's favorite directors, so it must have been a dream come true to have QT executive produce his second film—note that when our protagonists check in to the titular *Hostel* (2005), *Pulp Fiction* is playing on TV. *Hostel* is a notorious entry into the horror subgenre known as "torture porn," but it's a more intelligent movie than it gets credit for. Roth says it was modeled after a "slow-burn" horror movie, a subgenre that reaches some of its greatest heights in Takashi Miike's *Audition* (see chapter 4; Miike also makes a cameo in this movie as one of the patrons of Elite Hunting). People went into *Hostel* expecting it to be a nonstop onslaught of viscera, and were disappointed when the first thirty minutes played out more like an oddly serious National Lampoon movie. But Roth's deliberately messing with the audience's expectations. Those bros are condemning themselves to their fate with every pig-headed action in *Hostel*'s bloodless first half-hour...and what's a payoff without a setup, anyway?

Made on a budget of $4 million, *Hostel* went on to make over $20 million in its opening weekend and has spawned two sequels. *Hostel: Part II* (2007) was also directed by Roth and substitutes female backpackers Lauren German, Heather Matarazzo, and Bijou Phillips for the bros; a third installment went direct to video in 2011 without Roth's involvement and moves the action to Vegas...where it ought to stay.

Clint Eastwood in a *Fistful of Dollars* (United Artists/Photofest)

8

DJANGO UNCHAINED:
GOD FORGIVES ...I DON'T

> Once Upon a Time in the West, *I always loved it. It was almost like a film school in a movie for me. I watched it on TV as a kid and it really was great because it was like learning a certain directing style, it was Sergio Leone's style [laughs] but you could see how he used the camera.*
>
> —QUENTIN TARANTINO, *from* Once Upon a Time: Sergio Leone, 2001

If we're talking influences on the way Tarantino directs movies, forget noir, pulp, men on a mission, or any kind of -sploitation: spaghetti-Western master Sergio Leone trumps them all. As a kid, Tarantino would watch Leone's movies on TV and take notes. As early as *Pulp Fiction*, he cited Leone as an influence; *Kill Bill: Volume 2* was clearly inspired by Leone's particular brand of stylish Euro-Western; and now, Tarantino's making a spaghetti Western of his own in *Django Unchained*.

"Spaghetti Western" was born as an insult, concocted by contemptuous American critics in the 1960s to hurl at the wave of Westerns coming out of Europe. Classic Hollywood Westerns such as John Ford's *Stagecoach* (1939) saw nobility and moral uprightness in manifest destiny, but Sergio Leone and his cohorts (most notably "the other Sergio," Sergio Corbucci) saw the American West as a bleak and violent place driven by nihilistic greed. As Dan Edwards writes in his article on Leone for *Senses of Cinema*: "Hollywood Westerns had always invoked this dream of pure freedom only to subsume it by film's end under the sheen of domestic white 'civilization.' Leone, in contrast, dared to embrace the dream wholeheartedly ...Leone's camera celebrates the visceral energy of America's mythology of violent individualism while remaining coolly ambivalent about its morality."

Thus dubbed, spaghetti Westerns were dismissed as "trash" until relatively recently, as many film directors (not just Tarantino) have spoken openly and passionately about their love for the genre. You can argue all day about whether Clint Eastwood or John Wayne more accurately portrays how it "really was," but you can't deny, at least in retrospect, which one has had more staying power. After the spaghetti Westerns, even Hollywood, that bastion of everything mediocre, stopped making heroic Westerns in favor of revisionist works such as Clint Eastwood (himself a spaghetti Western star)'s *Unforgiven* (1992). And while most spaghetti Westerns were the stuff of grindhouses, at least the most famous one, *The Good, the Bad, and the Ugly* (1967), was a commercial success, and Ennio Morricone's soundtrack has since become shorthand for anything Old West. (You can't talk about Leone without talking about Ennio Morricone, the other half of what Tarantino calls "the best director-composer team in the history of film" and whose works have dominated the *Kill Bill: Volume 2* and *Inglourious Basterds* soundtracks.)

Leone was the most famous and successful spaghetti Western director, and his movie *A Fistful of Dollars* (1964) launched the genre. But there were hundreds of spaghetti Westerns released from its heyday in the mid-'60s until about a decade later (though by this point, spaghetti Westerns had descended into parodies, some intentional, some not). So while the spaghetti Western boom didn't last all that long, in that short amount of time, it managed to change our collective perception of the Old West for good.

For *Django Unchained*, Tarantino has taken the conventions of a spaghetti Western (such as Jamie Foxx and Christoph Waltz's master/pupil dynamic, a convention that appears in *For A Few Dollars More*, *Death Rides a Horse*, and *Day of Anger*, among others) and, being himself, has mashed them up with a Southern setting.

Adding flavor are elements of "racesploitation" pictures such as the shock-value classic *Mandingo*, an exercise in bad taste that only could have come from a transitional period in history like the '70s.

A FISTFUL OF DOLLARS

A Fistful of Dollars (1964) sets the template for Sergio Leone's "Dollars" trilogy, which in turn set the template for the entire spaghetti Western genre, but you've got to give credit where credit is due—*Fistful* wouldn't exist without *Yojimbo*. Leone and "the other Sergio," Sergio Corbucci, were both big fans of Akira Kurosawa's tale of a masterless samurai when it screened in Rome, and both began planning their own remakes. Imagine one Sergio calling up the other (it helps if you give them exaggerated cartoon pizza-mascot Italian accents):

"Sergio, did you see this movie *Yojimbo*?"

"Yes, Sergio! I'm even thinking of making a remake with gunfighters, a—how you say—Western, out of it."

"Ah, Sergio! I am also making a remake with the gunfighting!"

Oops. More on that later. Anyway, here's the storyline of *A Fistful of Dollars* and *Yojimbo* before it: A mysterious lone gunman arrives in a dusty desert town bitterly divided between two warring gangs. Being the enterprising type, this Man with No Name takes the advice of an innkeeper who tells him, "If you want to do some killing, you're sure to find somebody to pay you for it [here]." But our antihero approaches both sides to offer his services as a gun for hire, playing them against each other for his own personal gain.

Clint Eastwood plays The Man with No Name with a cocky smirk permanently smeared on his face, his signature olive-green (*not* brown) poncho on his back, and a foul-looking black cigarillo between his lips. According to Eastwood, he doesn't even smoke; he just puffed on the nasty things to get himself into a nasty frame of mind. (You'll get a similar vibe from Toshiro Mifune's burping, scratching, delightfully impudent title character in *Yojimbo*.) Incidentally, Eastwood's character technically *does* have a name in all three movies; in *Fistful*, he's Joe. The whole "Man with No

Name" mythos was a creation of marketing people trying to tie the three films together, but it was just so goddamn cool it stuck.

Fistful doesn't reach the glorious stylistic heights of Leone's later work, but even a minor Leone Western is much better than most. And even if it wasn't, it would still be worth your time for one reason: this is the first movie Sergio Leone did with Ennio Morricone. And if you've seen *Kill Bill: Volume 2*, you'll recognize the main theme—it's the swelling trumpet music that plays as Bud approaches Beatrix, who's lying on the ground outside his trailer with a chest full of rock salt.

FOR A FEW DOLLARS MORE

A nice thing about the "Dollars" trilogy is that the law of diminishing returns on sequels that affects most movies doesn't apply. *For a Few Dollars More* (1965) improves on *A Fistful of Dollars* with a more expansive story and more ambitious direction, and *The Good, the Bad, and the Ugly* is the best and most expansive of all.

For a Few Dollars More, the second film in the series, adds to the mix Lee Van Cleef, a veteran of American TV Westerns perpetually typecast as a villain. What else would you expect, with those beady, hawkish eyes and that sharp face? (Don't get me wrong, I *love* Lee Van Cleef ...and I'm not the only one. Check out the message board at TheBad.net for some of the more lustful tributes.) At least in spaghetti Westerns, Van Cleef had the opportunity to play antiheroes as well as villains. The ruthlessly efficient bounty hunter Colonel Douglas Mortimer, also known as The Man in Black, is one such antihero.

Mortimer teams up with The Man with No Name (still Clint Eastwood), known in this movie as Manco, Spanish for "one arm." Both Manco and Mortimer are after the same guy, a psychopathic killer named El Indio (Gian Maria Volonté). Here's how psycho El Indio is: he carries around a musical pocket watch that he stole from one of his victims, a woman who committed suicide after he raped her and killed her lover. He uses this morbid keepsake to count down his gun fights, telling the unlucky schmuck he's about to take out, "When the chimes finish, begin." As you can imagine, this evildoer has a large bounty on his head and quite a few wanted men in his posse. So Manco and Mortimer agree to work together and split the bounty on the entire gang, which will add up to quite a tidy sum…though as it turns out, Mortimer has an ulterior motive.

THE GOOD, THE BAD, AND THE UGLY

Here it is. The Holy Grail. The third film in Sergio Leone's "Dollars" trilogy, *The Good, the Bad, and the Ugly* (1966), the movie that Quentin Tarantino named as the greatest film of all time in a 2002 *Sight and Sound* poll. *The Good, the Bad, and the Ugly* is cinema stripped down to its most archetypal form, or as Roger Ebert puts it in his essay naming it one of his Great Movies: "Leone cares not at all about the practical or the plausible, and builds his great film on the rubbish of Western movie clichés, using style to elevate dreck into art…Leone's stories are a heightened dream in which everything is bigger, starker, more brutal, more dramatic, than life."

The heightened dream, the realer-than-real, the word we know blown up to mythic proportions: that's the kind of world Tarantino is creating to different degrees in all of his films. Leone is also a master of creating these worlds, and with *The Good, the Bad, and the Ugly*, he's created three larger-than-life characters, the kind of "simple, violent men" he saw in the history of America writ large on the movie screen.

First there's Blondie (once again, Clint Eastwood), his olive-green poncho now a dusty brown (he reportedly did not wash it once during the filming of all three "Dollars" movies). He's "The Good," though we already know that he's really not that much better than anyone else, just smarter and a better shot. Blondie has an interesting partnership with Tuco (Eli Wallach), full name Tuco Benedicto Pacífico Juan María Ramírez, but better known as "The Ugly"; though they're ostensibly partners throughout the entire movie, their relationship says ambivalent, defying the cliché that if two guys work together long enough in a movie, they'll inevitably become buddies. Tuco is a comical but dangerous wild card, a wanted bandit with whom Blondie strikes up an ingenious scam. Tuco is wanted all over the place, so Blondie trusses him up, turns him in, collects the reward money, then right as they're about to hang him, shoots down the noose so they can ride off to the next town and do it all over again. Finally, we've got Lee Van Cleef, professional movie bad guy, as a professional real-life bad guy, the clever, ruthless, and remorseless mercenary Angel Eyes, a.k.a. "The Bad." (Note that the music that plays when Angel Eyes first enters the movie is used in *Kill Bill: Volume 2* when we finally see Bill for the first time.)

All three of our protagonists are after a fortune in Civil War gold buried in a graveyard. One of them knows where the graveyard is, another knows the name on the grave, and you can be damned sure the third one wants to find out. This doesn't sound like much of a plot to hang a three-hour movie on, but the road to that final confrontation at Sad Hill Cemetery is a long and winding one, as Blondie and Tuco take turns abandoning one another in the desert to die, Angel Eyes becomes the leader of a Union POW camp where Tuco and Blondie are imprisoned, Blondie narrowly escapes being hanged when a bomb hits his hotel, and lots of other adventures.

The Good, the Bad, and the Ugly's influence reaches far beyond the spaghetti Western world; the title has entered into the English language as a figure of speech, and the soundtrack by Ennio Morricone is one of the best-known film scores ever. Period. Even people who have never seen the movie will recognize the theme, but the entire score, especially "The Ecstasy of Gold," is gorgeous, and sometimes the swelling of the soundtrack matches up with the vast empty landscape so beautifully it brings a tear to your eye.

It's an epic story that's got enough comedy, action, drama, and violence to make it a very quick 177 minutes (restored to its original Italian running time for the current DVD special edition, it was originally cut for the international market). And the climactic graveyard shootout is the absolute best, most mind-blowing movie standoff scene of all time, and the cinematography is a knockout, and Leone's at the absolute peak of his powers ... basically, if you don't already love *The Good, the Bad, and the Ugly*, then you need to start right now.

ONCE UPON A TIME IN THE WEST

After *The Good, the Bad, and the Ugly* became an international hit, Sergio Leone decided he wanted to try making something besides a Western for a change, only to find that movie producers' response to success is not "Go on, push your creative boundaries," but "Do the exact same thing that made us all that money last time." So when an offer of big Hollywood money and big Hollywood stars came Leone's way, it proved too good to refuse, and he said to himself, well...I'll let Tarantino explain that one: "It's like [Leone] said: 'This is your American Western, now I'm gonna subvert it, I'm gonna use your favorite good guy, Henry Fonda, and make him the bad guy.'"

Frank, Henry Fonda's character in *Once Upon a Time in the West* (1968), is a bad, *bad* dude, but in typical Leone antihero fashion, Frank's also our main character. Clint Eastwood, who had to be persuaded (i.e., offered more money) to even accept his role in *The Good, the Bad, and the Ugly*, declined the offer to play Fonda's nemesis, so Leone found a new nameless man: *The Dirty Dozen's* Charles Bronson. Bronson plays mysterious gunslinger and man of few words Harmonica, named for his penchant for playing the instrument (well *of course* he plays Ennio Morricone melodics; did you even have to ask?) rather than making small talk. And don't forget the majestic Claudia Cardinale as Jill McBain, a former New Orleans prostitute who's looking to start over out West. When Jill arrives at her new home in the desert outpost of Sweetwater, her homesteader husband and stepchildren are all dead, murdered by Frank and his gang. (Frank had been sent by a railroad magnate to intimidate McBain off his land before the railroad came through; when McBain refused, they killed his whole family.) Still, she decides to stay—where else would she go?—and falls under the protection of Harmonica, who is pursuing Frank for (you guessed it) his own reasons.

Leone's mastery of formal style is unmatched by this point, but he doesn't lay it on as thick as he did in *The Good, the Bad, and the Ugly*, favoring a more restrained approach. Leone hired Italian directors Dario Argento and Bernardo Bertolucci to help him with the screenplay, and the three were consciously quoting from American Westerns such as *High Noon* and *Shane*. *Once Upon a Time in the West* is a favorite of many film directors, not just Tarantino, including Martin Scorsese, George Lucas, John Carpenter, John Boorman, and Baz Luhrmann. And even though when it was first released a (heavily cut) version did poorly with audiences and critics, now it is considered by many the finest Western—and one of the finest films, period—ever made.

DJANGO

It took Sergio Corbucci two years longer than Sergio Leone to get his version of *Yojimbo* (see *A Fistful of Dollars*) onto the big screen, but the end result, *Django* (1966), is a darker, more sadistic, and arguably more stylish film. Franco Nero's Django cuts a more menacing figure than The Man with No Name in his mud-caked black duster, and even more mythic—Django doesn't ride a horse, meaning he *walked* through the desert dragging that coffin behind him on a chain. Yup, a coffin. And just you wait till you see what's in it!

After rescuing a prostitute, Maria (Loredana Nusciak), from a topless whipping in the desert, Django (Franco Nero) rides into a town controlled by two rival factions: a gang of racist KKK types in red hoods and a gang of gold-hungry Mexicans. And in true *Yojimbo* style, Django plays both sides against each other in order to get his hands on a cache of gold. Does he have an ulterior motive? Would there be a movie if he didn't?

Django really hammers home the death imagery—coffins, graveyards, crosses—intensifying in sadism as it goes along from the aforementioned topless whipping in the opening scene to the graphic, bloody maiming of Django's hands towards the end. It's muddy, it's melancholy, and it's morbid, but Corbucci makes it feel kitschy despite its nihilistic streak. *Django* is available on Blu-ray, a rare luxury for a non-Leone spaghetti Western, which allows you to absorb its muddy, overcast griminess in the most muddy, overcast, grimy way possible. Also rare is the option of watching the movie in English or Italian with English subtitles, each giving you a different impression of the film. Always the same, however, are the plaintive tones of the theme song, belted out by Roberto Fia (performing as Rocky Roberts): "Oh you've lost her, woah-oh, yeah you've lost her woah-*ooooh*/oh you've lost her forever, Django . . ."

Django is one of Tarantino's favorite films; Franco Nero recalled meeting him in Rome in a 2011 interview with the website *What Culture*: "Tarantino came to Rome and I had lunch with him. And he said, 'I was 14 when I started to watch your movies,' and he started to recite lines from my movies . . . he even remembered the music!"

The title of *Django Unchained* is most likely a nod to the wildly out-of-control phenomenon of unofficial *Django* sequels—or rather, of producers inserting the name "Django" into totally unrelated movies to boost box office. Django is played by a different actor in pretty much every one of these "sequels," with Franco Nero appearing only in *Django* and one "official" sequel, *Django Strikes Again* (1987), which plays more like a Rambo movie than the original. Official or not, they're of wildly differing quality, and some aren't even Westerns. As Nero explains in the *What Culture* interview, somehow in Germany, every single one of his movies became a Django movie: "In Germany they have a complex with Django," laughs Nero. "All the movies that I did they called them 'Django,' you know? Like my film *How to Kill a Judge*, a political thriller, became 'Django with the Mafia.' *The Shark Hunter* became 'Django versus the Shark'!"

So just because Tarantino's Django is played by Jamie Foxx, that doesn't mean he's not the "real" Django, because you see, there is no "real" Django. Django is whoever and whatever you say he is.

VIVA DJANGO

One of the legion of unofficial "Djangos"—*Viva Django!* (1967), alternately titled *Django, Get a Coffin Ready!*—is another favorite of Tarantino's (it made his list of Top 20 spaghetti Westerns on the seminal Spaghetti Western Database site). Terence Hill, a Franco Nero lookalike who later went on to great success as Trinity in the Trinity movies, is our Django in this one. Django has grown tired of the gunslinging lifestyle, so he's making tracks to California with his wife and a wagon full of gold, but before they can get there, bandits attack the convoy and kill Django's wife. It turns out that one of Django's former friends has double-crossed him, presumably because he doesn't know that if you double-cross Django, you're as good as dead.

Several years later, he's working as a hangman with a novel schtick...novel unless you've seen *The Good, the Bad, and the Ugly*, anyway: after sentencing men to death and stringing them up on the hangman's platform, he shoots down his charges at the last second. Django is gathering a private army of "phantoms"—criminals he has saved from death—with whom he will set out to get his final revenge. Will it be the end of the road for Django? Even if it is, don't worry about it—someone else will take up the role next time. An entertaining entry into the Django canon, *Viva Django* features lively action, good performances from its leads, and the fixation on morbid imagery without which a Django movie just wouldn't be a Django movie.

DEATH RIDES A HORSE

Speaking of death, "This is revenge, and there's nothing sweet about it!" screams the tagline for the unjustly obscure 1967 spaghetti Western *Death Rides a Horse*. And it certainly starts on a sour note: the first scene of *Death Rides a Horse* is more like a horror movie than a conventional Western as an entire family—including the kids—is murdered on a dark and stormy night on an isolated frontier settlement. But one of the children has managed to escape and is huddled outside in the rain, watching as the bad guys burn his house with the bodies of his relatives inside. (This particular sequence is remarkably similar to O-ren Ishii's origin story in *Kill Bill: Volume 1*.) At this moment, the boy, Bill Meceita, devotes his life to—say it with me now—Bloody. Fucking. Vengeance.

Fast-forward about fifteen years, and that little boy has grown into Aryan dreamboat John Phillip Law, whose resume also includes such awesome, crazy things as *Danger: Diabolik* and *Skidoo*. As Bill practices his shooting and dreams of getting his revenge, Ryan (Lee

Van Cleef) is released from prison after fifteen years of hard labor. Coincidence? Of course not. It doesn't take long for these two to cross paths, and Ryan helps Bill out of a jam in a great scene where Bill discovers that his poker partner is not just a dignified pillar of society, he's also (dum dum dummm) one of the men who killed his parents! When Bill finds out that Ryan is stalking the same men he is, he asks to accompany the seasoned gunfighter on his quest. Despite his initial distrust and dislike of the boy, Ryan eventually gives in and takes him under his wing. He could use some help getting his $10,000 back anyway...

Over time Ryan and Bill warm up to each other, but they never lose the ambivalence that a gunfighter needs to survive. Bill affectionately teases Ryan by calling him "Grandpaw," but double-crosses his mentor at the first opportunity, "just as you taught me." Later on Ryan shows up to help Bill out of another jam—he's been buried in sand up to his neck—but he takes his sweet time digging the kid out, making sure to work in a few jabs at his student while he does it. (Master and student were reunited in the '80s, when John Phillip Law and Lee Van Cleef, by then in his sixties and covering his bald spot with a cowboy hat, got back together for, of all things, a Midas commercial.)

The Leone influence in Giulio Petroni's direction is obvious in the juxtaposition of extreme long shots and extreme close-ups of shifty eyes and twitchy trigger fingers. One device that should get a smile from *Kill Bill* fans is Petroni's tendency to zoom in on the traumatized Bill's eyes every time he recognizes one of the killers, the screen turning blood red as the death of his family is superimposed over his face, a technique quoted liberally in *Kill Bill: Volume 1*. The theme, another predictably awesome Ennio Morricone creation, also appears in *Kill Bill: Volume 1* during the House of Blue Leaves massacre.

Despite its popularity in the US when it was first released, *Death Rides a Horse* has lapsed into the public domain as of 2012. However, the upside is that the lack of expensive rights clearances has led to its availability on an excellent restored, uncut DVD from Wild East, on Netflix Instant, and as a free (though poor quality) download on the US government public-domain media archive www.archive.org.

DAY OF ANGER

Lee Van Cleef stars once again as a hardened bounty hunter who takes a boy under his wing in the hard-to-find (but well worth it if you do) spaghetti Western *Day of Anger* (1967), directed by Tonio Valerii. Valerii served as assistant director on Sergio Leone's *For a Few Dollars More;* perhaps to avoid accusations of copycat-ism in *Day of Anger*, Valerii downplays the dramatic camerawork favored by his mentor for a less flashy but still remarkably well constructed style (especially in the gunfights, which utilize some very impressive multi-angle setups). In fact, *Day of Anger*'s only notable stylistic flourish is in the jazz-orchestra-meets-Morricone soundtrack by Riz Ortolani. (Like many of the films in this chapter, *Day of Anger*'s theme appeared in *Kill Bill: Volume 2*; it's very brief, but a snippet plays as Elle Driver takes a flying midair kick at Beatrix during their showdown in Bud's trailer.) The story, similarly, isn't particularly complex, leaving *Day of Anger*'s considerable appeal to rest on its classic theme of master and student.

Giuliano Gemma costars as Scott, the son of a prostitute who has spent his entire life sweeping floors, mucking out outhouses, and generally being spat upon by the residents of his hometown, Clifton. But Scott's fortunes change instantly and dramatically when lone gunman Frank Talby (Lee Van Cleef) rides into town. Talby makes quite an impression on the beleaguered young man—first, because he's the only person who has ever suggested that Scott should have the dignity of a last name (he adopts Mary, his mother's name), and second, because he kills one of Scott's tormenters in a duel. But Talby is just passing through, and so Scott mounts his trusty burro, Sartana (jokingly named after the hero of another series of spaghetti Westerns), and follows Talby out into the desert.

Talby's looking for Wild Jack (Al Mulock), a former co-conspirator who owes him $50,000 for a heist gone wrong. When he does find him, this unsavory fellow tells Talby the money is long gone. He too was double-crossed by their accomplices, three seemingly respectable residents of ... Clifton! So Talby heads back to where he came from, with Scott still tagging along like a pathetic puppy. But when Wild Jack ambushes Talby (What? He's a bad guy!) in the desert, and Scott proves himself useful in the ensuing gunfight, Talby finally agrees to take him on as a student. The newly minted sensei and student return to Clifton so Talby can get his revenge, though as we will see, his *real* role in that $50,000 robbery was not what he made it out to be. You see, Murph (Walter Rilla), a former sheriff turned stable boy and Scott's only friend, remembers the *last* time Talby came to town ...

Lee Van Cleef's performance in *Day of Anger* is wonderful. He's a confident, professional cold-blooded killer who takes pride in his "work," but he still has a softer side that comes out when he interacts with his student Scott. Thus he is able to combine both aspects of his onscreen persona—the wise, paternalistic voice of experience (Colonel Mortimer from *For a Few Dollars More*) and the self-serving sociopath (Angel Eyes from *The Good, the Bad, and the Ugly*)—into one fascinating character. Giuliano Gemma is also great as the vulnerable and confused Scott, an outcast who clearly covets Talby's calm self-assurance. Another great component of the movie is Talby's "lessons," where he teaches Scott the intricacies of the gunslinger's trade, which include sleight of hand and misdirection as well as a fast draw. *Day of Anger* has never had a proper DVD release in the US, but it pops up from time to time in repertory screenings and is available from the OOP (out of print) movies dealer CultCine.

NAVAJO JOE

"A Silhouette of Doom," Ennio Morricone's theme from *Navajo Joe* (1966), essentially functions as The Bride's theme song in *Kill Bill: Volume 2*. We first hear its rhythmic, suspenseful tones before the movie even starts in the precredits sequence, and again before The Bride's fight with Elle Driver; you'll also hear a section of a piece of music called "Demise of Barbara/Return of Joe" when (spoiler alert) Bill finally drops dead. Though it's a more obscure pick than some of the other films in this chapter, this "lesser" spaghetti

Western was still included on Tarantino's personal Top 20 for the Spaghetti Western Database.

A young Burt Reynolds, practically unrecognizable from the mustachioed ladies' man he personified later in his career, stars as the titular Navajo Joe, just one of many things the movie gets wrong about Navajos and Native Americans in general. (Like what? Navajos live in adobe houses, not teepees like they do in the movie; are accomplished weavers, who don't wear buckskins like they do in the movie; and are farmers, not migrant hunters like they are in the movie. It really ought to be called *Apache Joe*, if anything, but that doesn't rhyme.)

According to legend, Reynolds *hated* starring in this movie, which he considered beneath him and called "the worst experience" of his career. And according to the same legend, there was no love lost between the pouty star and director Sergio Corbucci, who reportedly drove Reynolds to the middle of the Almerian (Spanish) desert and left him there to make his own way back to set.

Anyway, Navajo Joe's mission of vengeance begins when a band of comancheros rides up to his village and starts pumping his peaceful Navajo kinfolk full of lead with their shotguns. And as these cold-blooded killers ride away, we spot a faraway figure on a mountaintop, watching them. Is it Navajo Joe? You know it! Is he going to get his revenge? You bet he is! *Navajo Joe* is inconsistent and definitely not Corbucci's best, but it's a respectable entry into the canon of hard-hitting bloody revenge movies that all of us—you, me, Tarantino—love so much.

THE GREAT SILENCE

The Great Silence (1968) is an unusual spaghetti Western in many respects, from its wintry setting (Utah during the blizzard of 1899) to its shocking ending (I can't give it away, obviously, but you'll *definitely* be talking about it afterward). It combines the cinematographic virtuosity of a Leone movie with a grisly Sergio Corbucci flair and a memorable Ennio Morricone score. Famous crazy person Klaus Kinski stars as the villainous bounty hunter Tigrero, also known as Loco. And here to end his reign of terror is Silence, played by French actor Jean-Louis Trintignant. Silence got his nickname after his throat was cut by bounty hunters when he was just a child, rendering him mute. He then took his hate and channeled it into becoming a bounty hunter who makes his living hunting other bounty hunters.

The problem with Loco is that he's in cahoots with the local justice of the peace, with whom he has a nice little scam going: he gets the justice to brand innocent townsfolk as criminals, giving him free rein to kill them and collect the bounty on their heads. See, this is the tail end of the lawless era in the West, and a new sheriff is on his way to replace Loco as the arbiter of justice in this snowy mountain town. Seeing that his income opportunities are about to dry up, Loco is looking to cash in (i.e., kill as many people as possible) while he still can. So Pauline (Vonetta McGee), a young African American homesteader whose husband recently found himself on Loco's death list, sends for Silence to silence Loco.

The Great Silence is a very grim tale perfectly suited to its frost-bitten surroundings. The line between good and evil gets very murky at times, and Silence himself is like an apparition, like a ghost story whispered around the campfire on a cold, windy night. As Pauline explains: "Once, my husband told me of this man. He avenges our wrongs. And the bounty killers sure do tremble when he appears. They call him 'Silence.' Because wherever he goes, the silence of death follows."

Awesome, right?

THE MERCENARY

The subgenre of spaghetti Westerns known as "Zapata Westerns" combines the violent action that all spaghetti Westerns share with a liberal (pun intended) dose of left-wing politics under the pretense of the Mexican Revolution of 1910 to 1920. Sergio Leone made an entry into the subgenre with *Duck, You Sucker!*, a.k.a. *A Fistful of Dynamite* (1971), but "the other Sergio"— Sergio Corbucci, who can never resist working a political angle into his stories (it's not a coincidence that Django fights the KKK)—is its master. The first Zapata Western, and one of the harder ones to find, is *The*

Mercenary (Il Mercenario), a.k.a. *A Professional Gun* (1968), starring the spaghetti Western all-star trio of Franco Nero, Tony Musante, and Jack Palance. The sunny Mexican setting, complete with lovely desert sunsets that glow purple and orange, stands in sharp contrast to *The Great Silence*, which Corbucci released the same year; the brisk, energetic, occasionally outrageous tone is also markedly different from that thoroughly pessimistic film. The cherry on top is the movie's distinctive whistled theme, "L'Arena"—in my humble opinion, the most beautiful of all Ennio Morricone themes. ("L'Arena" features prominently, like so many other Morricone compositions, in *Kill Bill: Volume 2*; you can hear it when Bud nails The Bride's coffin shut, and again when she escapes from the grave.)

Franco Nero (a.k.a. "Django," the role that would haunt him his entire career) plays Sergei Kowalski, or as everyone in the movie calls him, "The Polack." We don't know where The Polack comes from exactly (probably Poland) or why he's so damn good at fighting. But we do know that he's a professional mercenary who cares about no one but himself, a trait that's reflected in his tendency to strike the matches for his cigars on other peoples' teeth, hats, boots...even a lady's cleavage!

Most of the movie is told in flashback as Kowalski, sitting in the stands at a circus performance, tries to remember why he recognizes the circus clown in the arena below. Turns out that that clown is his comrade-in-arms Paco Roman (Tony Musante), a revolutionary leader who teamed up with Kowalski after the mercenary offered to let the "companeros" use his new toy—a machine gun—to fight the Mexican army...for a fee, of course. After parting ways with Paco and his men, Kowalski is ambushed in the desert by the bloodthirsty bandit Curly (Jack Palance, one of a small group of actors who could say they were more typecast than Lee Van Cleef), but Paco and his gang pass by just in time to humiliate Curly and kill his men. So Paco, still high on his victory over the regiment, makes a proposition to Kowalski: will he stay and help them fight *la revolucion?* Ever easygoing and seeing dollar signs, Kowalski accepts.

Full of double-crosses, near-misses, and daring escapes, *The Mercenary* is able to take on politics without taking itself too seriously. Take the climactic gun duel in the bullfighting ring: it's a tense Mexican standoff as our three heroes face each other in the ring, guns drawn, "L'Arena" swelling on the soundtrack, the tension pulled tight enough to snap . . . oh, and Paco's still dressed like a clown. *The Mercenary* is sadly quite difficult to find on DVD, though if you have Netflix Instant, you can stream it there, and it plays occasionally in repertory theaters.

Two years later, Corbucci reunited with Franco Nero for *Compañeros* (*Vamos a matar, Compañeros*); it's part sequel and part remake of *The Mercenary*, except that this one is less of a political epic and more of a buddy comedy with a revolution just coincidentally going on around it. This time Franco Nero plays a Swede, not a Polack, though he's still the same cocky bastard; Thomas Milan steps into the sidekick role as Vasco, a former bandit who is converted to the revolutionary cause by the wise Professor Xantos (Fernando Rey). Jack Palance also returns as basically the same character, but with a twist—he's still a lone bandit and an amoral psycho, but in this one he's also a pothead!

RIO BRAVO

Depending on when you ask, Tarantino will name the 1959 John Wayne/Dean Martin Western *Rio Bravo* as either his #1 or #2 favorite movie of all time. He likes it so much that he even uses it as a litmus test for women: as he famously said in the November 1994 issue of *Rolling Stone*, "When I'm getting serious about a girl, I show her *Rio Bravo* and she better fucking like it." Hey, why not? *Rio Bravo* is a classic story about the power of loyalty, love, and redemption, and why would you want to date someone who isn't interested in that?

Rio Bravo comes courtesy of master director Howard Hawks (see chapter 2, *The Big Sleep*). After the box-office flop *Land of the Pharaohs* put him off filmmaking for four long years, this celebrated movie marked a massive comeback for Hawks, a giant of the "Golden Age" of Hollywood who worked in many genres and conquered them all. *Rio Bravo* was Hawks's second time working with John Wayne, then at the height of his blue-eyed, wide-stanced popularity. Westerns dominated the then-newfangled medium of television at the time, and Hawks observed that viewers tuned in week after week to spend time with the characters, not to follow the plot, and so he set out to craft a character-based Western.

Chance (Wayne) is a frontier sheriff in small-town Texas who holds court over jesters "Stumpy" (Walter Brennan), a toothless old man; and Dude (Martin) (or as the locals call him, "Borachon," Spanish for "drunk"), who turned to the bottle to soothe the pain of a broken heart. Enter "Rocky" Ryan, a.k.a. "Colorado" (Ricky Nelson), a baby-faced gunfighter (maybe a little too baby-faced; he seems like he would be more at home at a sock hop than a gunfight) who rides into town with a wagon train. The leader of that wagon train suggests that maybe Chance could use some more deputies, proving his point by getting gunned down in the street shortly thereafter. Chance tries to hold the murderer, the brutish Joe Burdette (Claude Akins) until the US Marshal can come and pick him up, but Joe's powerful and bull-headed brother, Nathan (John Russell), wants him free by any means necessary. Outnumbered and outgunned, Chance finally agrees to take on Colorado as a deputy.

Unlike the bleak, mercenary attitude of movies such as *The Great Silence* or *Day of Anger*, *Rio Bravo* is full of good-natured optimism that's reflected in Dude's redemptive character arc and in John Wayne, just doing his thing as the quintessential good guy. Self-control is the key to Wayne's persona, not unconstrained violence (This is probably a reflection of Wayne's technique, which was largely based on reacting to the other actors.) In *Rio Bravo* the only thing that really gets under Chance's skin is "Feathers" (Angie Dickinson), a brassy lady gambler with a flirtatious streak; at first she's just passing through town, but she decides to stay just to drive Chance crazy, abuse he's happy to take from a gal like her.

Rio Bravo ambles along at a leisurely 141 minutes, and a lot of that time is spent on character development; we never actually leave the confines of the town, composed mostly of the jail, the hotel where Feathers works, and the street in between. If you're used to hyperactive contemporary action movies, that might seem like an eternity, but let me point out that that's a full fifteen minutes shorter than *Transformers: Dark of the Moon,* and I bet at least some of y'all saw *Transformers: Dark of the Moon.* Let's compare the two: *Rio Bravo* has great performances, a genuinely touching story, and masterful direction, and *Transformers* has confusing CGI action, an affectless Victoria's Secret model, and a jive-talking robot.

I think I might have just made *Rio Bravo* a deal breaker too.

BOSS, A.K.A. *BOSS NIGGER*

In 1972 and 1973, Fred Williamson starred in a pair of movies, *The Legend of Nigger Charley* and *The Soul of Nigger Charley,* which attempted to cash in on the blaxploitation and spaghetti Western trends simultaneously by dropping defiant black heroes into Old West settings. It's a great concept, marrying all those cool Western tropes with funky blaxploitation style, but the best results came when Williamson took it upon himself to pen a third movie, *Boss Nigger* (now known only as *Boss*), released in 1975.

As you can see from the title, *Boss* pulls no punches in the racial-slur department, including the titular theme song by Leon Moore, which is appropriately soulful and highly hummable, though use your discretion about randomly singing it in public. In addition to the song, the racial dialogue throughout the movie is very highly charged; they probably use the word *nigger* about two hundred times. Ironically, it's pretty tame in other aspects and was originally released in theaters with a PG rating, although that one word alone would put it solidly into R territory today. But before you start getting nervous, take a deep breath and try to remember that just because a movie depicts racism, that doesn't make it racist. Before you get offended by the "N-word" in *Boss,* you have to take into account the climate in which it was made (the pre-PC '70s), the time period it's set in (the way, wayyyyy pre-PC Old West), and how the word is used in the movie itself. Sure, that guy may have just called Fred Williamson a "nigger" to his face, but now Williamson's going to outdraw that narrow-minded motherfucker and show him who the real man is. Think of it like the ending of *Inglourious Basterds*: it's cinematic revenge as historical wish fulfillment.

Anyway, Williamson stars as the uberfunky Boss, with blaxploitation regular D'Urville Martin as his sidekick Amos. Both are former slaves turned sharp-dressed bounty hunters (Williamson's leather Shaft coat and gigantic belt buckle are particularly anachronistic), bad motherfuckers who clearly relish the role reversal. As Amos tells a white politician, "Y'all have been hunting black folks so long, we wanted to see what it's like hunting white folks." Boss and Amos roll into a new town full (as always) of racist settlers, and finding the sheriff and sheriff's deputy positions vacant, volunteer themselves for the positions. Since they can clearly outgun any man in town, the townsfolk vote against their own prejudices and approve the measure.

Boss and Amos set about establishing "Black Law," which includes feeding the poor Mexican children living on the outskirts of town (a measure that is, believe it or not, controversial) and a provision against using one of the words in the title (hint: it's not *boss*). However, the mayor is in cahoots with the very same thug, escaped convict Jed Clayton (William Smith), that Boss and Amos came to town looking for in the first place. Our heroes pose a double threat to the bigoted Jed, so he's going to give them trouble by terrorizing the town's minorities... but trouble's nothing Boss and Amos can't handle. *Boss* is an amusing and action-packed revenge fantasy, and although it's clearly low budget and occasionally fizzles out during the action scenes, you can tell that Fred Williamson and D'Urville Martin are having a lot of fun. Don't be put off by the title, and you may like it a whole lot more than you expected to.

See also: *Skin Game*, a 1971 comedy-Western starring James Garner and Louis Gossett Jr. as a bounty hunter and a free black man in the antebellum South who have devised a scheme that would make Tuco and Blondie proud. Garner pretends to be a down-on-his-luck owner who needs to sell his slave (Gossett) for some extra cash. But after driving up the bidding and "selling" Gossett for a healthy sum, the men split town, meeting up later to split the profits.

HELLO, UNCLE TOM:
FIVE "RACESPLOITATION" MOVIES TO OFFEND
AND ASTOUND

Quentin pays homage to a lot of different genres. He would like to say it's a spaghetti Western, and I guess in ways, it is. [But] when you start talking about Farewell Uncle Tom *and some of the other derivative films of that era—*Mandingo*—those things play in there too. It's his take on those films, but it's not like it's not part of the fabric of this country, and it happened. We'll deal with it as honestly and as Tarantino-esque as we can.*

—SAMUEL L. JACKSON *on preparing for his role in* Django Unchained, Hollywood Reporter *interview, 2012*

5. *THE INTRUDER*

In 1962, B-movie producer Roger Corman decided to take a break from cheesy horror flicks and direct a *serious* movie, an "issues picture" that would confront the reality of racism in America head-on. The result—alternately titled *Shame* and *I Hate Your Guts*, depending on whether it was playing a Northern city or a Southern drive-in—was one of the only Corman pictures (out of 401 and counting) to lose money. Needless to say, Roger never went "serious" again. If you're a fan of William Shatner or are looking for that special something to spice up your found-footage mix, look it up on YouTube (or www.archive.org, where it's available under the title *Shame*) for the surreal sight of Captain Kirk delivering KKK-worthy stump speeches.

4. *WHITE DOG*

From master of gritty social realism Sam Fuller (see chapter 2) comes *White Dog* (1982), a movie deemed so incendiary that its release in America was suppressed until late 2008, when the Criterion Collection released it on DVD. *White Dog* was based on a true story about *Breathless* star Jean Seberg, who adopted a dog that turned out to be a "white dog," or a dog trained to attack African Americans on sight. Ironically, the studio suppressed its release based on rumors that the movie itself was racist, though when you actually see it, it's obviously not. What it is, is a blunt indictment of prejudice that asks: is racism curable, or a terminal condition?

3. DRUM

The poster for *Drum* (1976) screams that this is the movie that "out-Mandingos *Mandingo*!" And yeah, it's got even more nudity and outrageous scenarios than its predecessor. In the end though, it's less disturbing, simply because it's a more typical exploitation movie. Topless women getting whipped? Yawn. But after the steamy, sexually depraved aura that surrounds *Mandingo* like a sweaty glove, it's kind of a relief to have some sleaziness that you actually have a reference point for. Plus in this one, Ken Norton is permitted to deliver actual lines of dialogue!

2. MANDINGO

Unbelievably politically incorrect and difficult to find on DVD, *Mandingo* (1975) seems like a transmission from another galaxy when you watch it today. It's hard to believe it was produced by a major studio and played all over the country in the '70s, but like *Ilsa, She-Wolf of the SS*, there's something so scuzzy and, dare I say it, ballsy about *Mandingo* that you don't *dare* look away. There's something to offend everybody here: if the wall-to-wall racial slurs and mistreatment of slaves (including using little black children as footstools) doesn't get you, maybe the tawdry sexuality and blatant objectification of both women and men (star Ken Norton is treated like a side of beef throughout) will. Mede (Norton) is a fighting slave, a "Mandingo" who is bought and brought to a plantation where the master (James Mason) has a taste for black "wenches," much to the chagrin of his embittered wife Susan George. As an act of retaliation, the Missus takes the studly new acquisition as her personal bed slave, an arrangement that obviously isn't going to work out for anybody.

1. GOODBYE UNCLE TOM

Goodbye Uncle Tom (1971) presents itself as an "educational docu mentary," but that's like saying *Deep Throat* is a "sex-ed video." On the flimsiest of pretexts—directors Gualtiero Jacopetti and Franco Prosperi claim to *actually go back in time* to record the horrors of slavery—we're presented with a nonstop parade of violent racist ideology and stomach-churningly graphic scenes of rape, humiliation, torture, and grotesque medical experimentation inflicted on slaves by their masters. (*Goodbye Uncle Tom* was shot in Haiti with the blessing of dictator François "Papa Doc" Duvalier, no slouch in the torture department himself.) The movie caused quite a stir upon its initial release and was slapped with an X rating for being "far more sexually explicit and perverted than conventional pornography," no doubt leaving amoral distributors giddy at all the free publicity. *Goodbye Uncle Tom*'s only redeeming quality is that this is all based on real events from the historical record, forcing the viewer to confront this dark chapter in American history head-on.

APPENDIX A:
ROLLING THUNDER PICTURES

I said, "Harvey, I'm the best acquisition guy you've got. You should just let me release four films a year. We'll pay a low amount for them, and it'll be like a specialty label inside Miramax. And it won't cost you a thing."... That was the original idea behind Rolling Thunder. Now I don't want to release new films so much as older exploitation movies and give them a new life... We're here to bring back the glory of '70s chopsocky movies, Italian crime films, blaxploitation—we'll get a spaghetti Western in there eventually.
—QUENTIN TARANTINO talks about Rolling Thunder Pictures, *LA Weekly* interview, June 14, 1997

It's too bad Tarantino never got the chance to release a spaghetti Western—that would have been awesome. But alas, after only two years in existence, Tarantino's pet VHS/DVD label was shut down by the powers that be at Miramax, citing poor sales for the titles that had already been released. If you're looking to catch up on the Rolling Thunder catalog (each of which can be considered a personal recommendation from Tarantino), this poor performance has its upside. Although they are technically out of print, Rolling Thunder releases can still be easily located at video stores or on major e-commerce sites such as Amazon.com for a reasonable price.

THE BEYOND *(1981), dir. Lucio Fulci*
See chapter 5.

CHUNGKING EXPRESS *(1994), dir. Wong Kar-Wai*

A dreamy, impressionistic meditation on love and longing from Hong Kong's most swooningly romantic director. You'll never hear "California Dreamin'" by the Mamas and the Papas quite the same way again. Also available on DVD and Blu-ray from The Criterion Collection.

CURDLED *(1996), dir. Reb Braddock*

Pitch-black comedy starring Angela Jones (a.k.a. "the cabbie from *Pulp Fiction*") as a Columbian immigrant in Miami with a murder scrapbook and a gig as a crime-scene cleaning lady. Highly recommended for *Dexter* fans.

DETROIT 9000 *(1973), dir. Arthur Marks*

See chapter 3.

HARD CORE LOGO *(1996), dir. Bruce McDonald*

Technically a "mockumentary," but don't expect *This Is Spinal Tap*–type goofiness (though it does have some very funny moments) from this fake Canadian documentary about a punk band's contentious reunion tour.

MIGHTY PEKING MAN *(1977), dir. Meng-Hwa No*

This thoroughly silly interpretation of the King Kong story comes courtesy of Hong Kong's famous Shaw Brothers Studios and features sub-Gargantuas special effects and bottle-blonde jungle queen Evelyne Kraft spinning in slow motion with a leopard draped around her shoulders. A perfect midnight movie.

SONATINE *(1993), dir. Takeshi Kitano*

"Beat" Takeshi doing his stony-faced ultraviolent yakuza thing as only he can. Nobody plays sardonic like Beat, especially with loaded gun in hand.

SWITCHBLADE SISTERS *(1975), dir. Jack Hill*

See chapter 6.

APPENDIX B:
THE BEST OF QT–FEST

Every year from 1997 to 2001 and again in 2005, Quentin Tarantino brought 16mm and 35mm prints from his extensive personal collection to the Alamo Drafthouse, Austin, Texas's famous "church" for cinema lovers. The result was QT-Fest, a week of eating, sleeping, and breathing movies with Tarantino himself introducing and discussing every film with the audience. In 2006 he brought back the best of the bunch for a special "Best of" edition. If the movies in this book are cinema's "greatest hits" for Tarantino fans, then consider these the deep cuts:

BEST OF QT-FEST 2006

Kiss the Girls and Make Them Die (1966), dir. Henry Levin,
　　Arduino Maiuri
Snake in the Monkey's Shadow (1979), dir. Sam Cheung
The Savage Seven (1968), dir. Richard Rush
Hollywood Man (1976), dir. Jack Starrett
Wipeout (**a.k.a.** *The Boss*) (1973), dir. Fernando Di Leo
Brotherhood of Death (1976), dir. Bill Berry III
The Gravy Train (**a.k.a.** *The Dion Brothers*) (1974),
　　dir. Jack Starrett
The Outfit (1974), dir. John Flynn
Billy Jack (1971), dir. Tom Laughlin
Vanishing Point (1971), dir. Richard Sarafian
Rolling Thunder (1977), dir. John Flynn
The Blood-Spattered Bride (1972), dir. Vicente Aranda

Twisted Nerve (1968), dir. Roy Boulting

Don't Go in the House (1980), dir. Joseph Ellison

Policewomen (1974), dir. Lee Frost

Hell Night (1981), dir. Tom DeSimone

The Legend of the Wolf Woman (1976), dir. Rino di Silvestro

Pretty Maids All in a Row (1971), dir. Roger Vadim

The Girl from Starship Venus (1975), dir. Derek Ford

INDEX

INDEX

If You Like Series

The If You Like series plays the game of cultural connectivity at a high level—each book is written by an expert in the field and travels far beyond the expected, unearthing treats that will enlighten even the most jaded couch potato or pop culture vulture.

If You Like the Beatles...
Here Are Over 200 Bands, Films, Records, and Other Oddities That You Will Love
by Bruce Pollock
Backbeat Books
978-1-61713-018-2 • $14.99

If You Like Metallica...
Here Are Over 200 Bands, CDs, Movies, and Other Oddities That You Will Love
by Mike McPadden
Backbeat Books
978-1-61713-038-0 • $14.99

If You Like Monty Python...
Here Are Over 200 Movies, TV Shows, and Other Oddities That You Will Love
by Zack Handlen
Limelight Editions
978-0-87910-393-4 • $14.99

If You Like the Terminator...
Here Are Over 200 Movies, TV Shows, and Other Oddities That You Will Love
by Scott Von Doviak
Limelight Editions
978-0-87910-397-2 • $14.99

If You Like the Sopranos...
Here Are Over 150 Movies, TV Shows, and Other Oddities That You Will Love
by Leonard Pierce
Limelight Editions
978-0-87910-390-3 • $14.99

If You Like Led Zeppelin...
Here Are Over 200 Bands, Films, Records, and Other Oddities That You Will Love
by Dave Thompson
Backbeat Books
978-1-61713-085-4 • $16.99

If You Like Quentin Tarantino...
Here Are Over 200 Films, TV Shows, and Other Oddities That You Will Love
by Katherine Rife
Limelight Editions
978-0-87910-399-6 • $16.99

Prices, contents, and availability subject to change without notice.